Stephanie -
Enjoy the Chase!

Tracy Line

CHASING GOD

Finding Faith from the Outside Looking In

Tracy Line

Hawthorne Publishing

Credit for the cover image; Cover Image: iStock.com

ISBN: 978-0-9912095-9-0

Manufactured in the United States of America

Hawthorne Publishing
15601 OakRoad
Carmel, IN 46033
317-867-5183

www.hawthornepub.com

Dedication

To my parents, John and Sue Beard, and to my family,
Steve, Sarah, Megan and Abby. I love you more than you
can imagine.

Table of Contents

CHILDHOOD MUSINGS

PRACTICING WHAT I PREACH

ALTERED FAITH

Preface

For as long as I can remember I have believed in God. And while many Christians have had times of doubting his existence over the course of their lives, I have not. There have been times when I wondered, but I could never really, truly believe he wasn't there.

It's not because my parents told me to believe; they didn't.

It's not because I was raised in a church; I wasn't.

It's not because I experienced tragedy and found God in the midst of it; this is not my story.

My story is one of a young girl who at age four decided to tell Jesus she believed in him while sitting alone on her bed in her room on a random afternoon of play. From that day forward, God held her hand and never, ever let go. Even as she didn't go church, even as she barely gave God a thought, even as she rarely prayed, she continued to believe. And because of that, God never let go of her. Instead, he pursued her, imprinted himself upon her heart, and waited patiently for her to draw slowly closer to him.

My now-strong faith was years in the making. Understanding the ideas and ways of a Christian life, becoming comfortable with it: this did not happen overnight. Instead I inched my way forward ever so slowly, baby steps followed by baby steps followed by more awkward and uncomfortable baby steps.

This book is about my journey. From watching Jim and Tammy Faye Bakker on the couch in my basement as a child, to learning what a Christian is, to realizing men and women of God fail him and do so often; these were all steps in my passage. I know no step was aimless, no stop along the way without purpose. Everything I am now is because of where God has led me.

As I transitioned from being secular to the occasional churchgoer to a daily chaser of faith, my quality of life has improved. I am happier, more at peace, and life itself feels more meaningful. My hope is that this book will encourage you in your own walk of faith. My personal journey in faith raises three important questions for readers to consider:

Does consistent church attendance and participation during childhood aid in one's choosing to practice Christianity as an adult?

How do changes in the worldview of Christianity and in our own American culture affect the beliefs and actions of modern Christians?

With fewer people attending church than ever, how can Christians encourage others in their journey to faith, even if they have never before been exposed to the church?

Whether you are just curious, a believer who hasn't thought much beyond church on Sunday or a lifelong fan of all things God, I hope you know God is there, available to you any time, anywhere. I pray my stories will entertain, inspire and help you find love, joy and peace in your own life. God bless.

Just So You Know…

Chasing God is a creative work of nonfiction. The events and descriptions in this book are true and are accounted for based on my memory, which is by all means flawed. Certain conversations and some of the descriptive details required a bit of filling in the gaps. I did my best.

Everything I've written here is true, but it may not be entirely factual. In some cases I have compressed events and combined two people into one. I have changed the names of many of the characters.

CHILDHOOD MUSINGS

Finding God in a 19-inch Black Box

I am in the basement, sitting on my family's Sears and Roebuck black, white and green plaid sofa. It is a cold day in Indiana, and the air holds a slight mustiness to it, so common in the basements of the 1970s. Because I am only four years old, my toes don't even reach the end of the sofa cushions.

I am comfortable here, alone in my basement. My father has turned it into a rec room for the family. Behind the couch sits our pool table, and to the right of that a bar my father constructed out of plywood paneling. Nice idea, but it never got used.

The basement was a labor of love for my father. Besides the bar, he also paneled all four walls of the room and added a drop ceiling. On one wall he left a cut-out for our TV so it would appear built in. For as hard as he worked, the furniture was still slightly worn, the rug beneath the couch a tad dirty, and the entire room was cold. But it was ours, particularly my brother's and mine, and we loved it.

I'm here again, in my mind.

In my lap sits a big bowl of buttered popcorn, compliments of my mother, an adjunct college professor, who is upstairs grading papers while I watch TV. I am devouring my snack while glued to the television, watching Jim and Tammy Faye Bakker, hosts of *The 700 Club*. Tammy's eyelashes both fascinate and confuse me. Regardless, I'm in awe.

The 700 Club, a live Christian-themed talk show, originally aired in 1961 and has graced various channels of television ever since. Jim and Tammy Faye Bakker were the original hosts. The show typically started out with the Bakkers welcoming their audience, and then one or the other would interview the guests, who would give a testimony to their Christian faith. I would sit riveted as I heard men and women of various ages talk about how Satan tried to ruin their lives, but that God was right there, waiting in the wings to bring them to the light. In between the talking was a lot of singing; Tammy herself often sang.

So yes, at age four, while other kids were watching cartoons, I was watching the Bakkers. Why? Good question. This show was certainly not one others in my family embraced; in fact, I'm not sure my mom ever knew I watched it. My afternoons in the basement with Jim and Tammy were all my own, a place to relax after a tough day of preschool.

There were many things I loved about *The 700 Club*, and none of them had to do with the content of the show. For one thing, I was drawn in by Jim and Tammy's enthusiasm (real or perceived? I'm not sure now). Jim exuded such gratitude; he blessed the day, blessed the guests, blessed the people supporting the show. It was all so positive and made me feel happy inside. Tammy, with her bright red lipstick, bouffant blond hair, and thick eyelashes, was almost scary to a four-year-old, yet she too, had an air about her. Her love for the Lord seemed real to me. She really came alive while belting out those gospel tunes. While the Bakkers had much trouble to come later in life (Jim spent time in prison for embezzlement from the show), I still believe their faith was genuine. I presume at some point fame and fortune changed them and eventually, I can only hope, sent them back the other way again.

While I loved Jim and Tammy's enthusiasm for the Lord, I found the guests and their stories confusing. Guest after guest would tell his story, emphatically carrying on about how lost he was, how depression or alcohol or Satan gripped him. But he was lucky: Jesus came to the rescue. Tammy would ooh and ah, nodding and sighing as she listened to the testimonies. She would often tear up. With the infinite wisdom of a four-year-old, I felt Tammy Faye must be the most caring person on Earth. And who was this Jesus character?

I connected with these stories, though they worried me a bit. My family attended a large Baptist church when I was very young, but my memories of it are scarce. I know I went to Sunday school a few times, but there was little about Jesus, and Satan was never brought up. What if Satan had me in his grasp? What if I fell into a pit and couldn't get out? Would this Jesus fellow save me? I wasn't sure, but I knew Jim and Tammy would be there for me.

In watching these individuals tell their stories, I determined, with my child's mind, that there were two sets of people on this earth. People who had found Jesus were calm, happy and seemingly problem-less. Then there was the rest of us: people who were just getting by like me and worrying about whether there really was a witch in her closet or spiders under the covers in her bed. And in the year 1969, to a tiny, shy little girl, one who harbored fears of strangers and getting in trouble at preschool, *The 700 Club* and the Bakkers brought a sense of hope.

If I could find what the people on that TV show had, everything would be okay. I could be happy and peaceful and Satan wouldn't stand a chance. Whatever they had, I wanted, too. I started by doing just as Jim had told me: I asked Jesus to live in my heart.

Eventually I grew up and grew bored with *The 700 Club*. Every episode seemed the same. But that wasn't the end of my relationship with the televangelists. In the mid-'70s, when I was ten or eleven, Robert Schuller became my new hero. While Dad mowed the grass and Mom buried herself in the newspaper, I spent my Sunday mornings watching *The Hour of Power* (luckily for me, this was in the pre-cable era, no hundreds of channels from which to choose). And in my ten-year-old mind, Robert Schuller was The Man.

With his broad smile, bright blue eyes and deep, resounding voice, Schuller was a powerhouse in the age of televangelism. He wore a pastor's robe, not a grey pinstriped polyester suit like Jim Bakker, and there was no bouffant-haired blond at his side. Schuller had an air of credibility. He was authoritative. When he tossed his head back, closed his eyes, put his hands to the sky and said with his deep baritone voice, "Jesus loves you!" by God, you believed him.

I had so much to learn from this man! And I trusted him completely. I guess it's even fair to say, though I'm embarrassed to admit it, that in my own way, I loved him. Robert Schuller was God incarnate to me. He told me God loved me. He told me I could do anything. No matter what the world told me, Robert Schuller made me believe I mattered.

It didn't take long for me to write to him. Each week, at the end of the show, the cameras would move from the pulpit to another staff member of the show who would tell you how you could support Dr. Schuller and his ministry. You were invited to write to tell him how God had worked in your life and include your 501-C-3 tax-free donation. This man had helped me believe in myself. I owed it to him to tell him that. Plus, one thing Dr. Schuller, a master marketer, offered was this: free gifts.

In the last ten minutes of the show, when they asked for the donation, some trinket or another would be showcased. It might be a small book, a knickknack for your desk or even a Christmas ornament. All you had to do was write and ask for the gift, and if you wanted to donate money to cover the cost of the gift, well, that would be okay, too. But either way, you got the goods.

What I said in my initial letter now escapes me, but I would guess my ten-year-old self wrote to tell him I liked his show. Wrote to tell him he was a really good preacher. Wrote to let him know he made me believe in myself. And he responded—with marketing materials (and my free gift).

The solicitations from *The Hour of Power* scared me. From them I learned that without proper funding, the show could be cancelled at any time! CANCELLED? What then? If not Robert Schuller, who would tell me I mattered? Who would remind me that I was capable of so much more? I could not let this happen.

These slick brochures showing colorful images of Dr. Schuller in the pulpit, inspirational messages printed over fields of flowers and large sophisticated graphs detailing the costs to keep him on the air drew me in. Could I help? Could I give what I had to ensure they could pay for the next TV spot? At least once, I sent him some change taped to my note in an envelope. Even when I realized the same threat for cancellation came every single week, that the show could likely manage without my donation, the marketing never offended me. I liked getting his mail. Large, colorful envelopes stuffed with...hope. Hope that someday I would really believe what he was telling me. The letters were physical reminders of Schuller's famous message of possibility thinking. Seeing the words on paper as I ripped open each envelope led to the words settling in my heart. Maybe it was really true, I'd think. Maybe one day I might really discover I had it in me to achieve whatever it was I wanted in life.

I can't tell you how many Robert Schuller *Hour of Power* gifts I collected over the years. I sent away for the medallion with an eagle on one side and the Twenty-Third Psalm on the other. I sent away for a daily devotional book. Each Christmas, I looked forward to the ornament he offered for that specific year. I accumulated multiple Christmas ornaments. And here's a little secret: I still have a few of them.

The gifts meant so much to me. I was a shy child, so unsure of myself and apparently in great need for someone to remind me over and over and over again that I mattered (my parents must have had no credibility in this arena). I rarely sent donations for the gifts. But no worries—when I got to be about eleven, I supported the ministry through the purchase of his books, many of which topped the best-seller list.

I read *You Can Be the Person You Want to Be*. I read *Peace of Mind through Possibility Thinking*. I read *Be Happy You are Loved*. Safe to say, I was a devoted fan of this televangelist. He was so full of energy, bursting with life, a true force to be reckoned with. Each week I watched the show, angst filling my heart when once again I learned that if they didn't get X amount of dollars that week, the show was in jeopardy of going off the air. But God was good: the *Hour of Power* continued long after my childhood.

While they must have thought it odd, my parents said little about the packages I was receiving in the mail, or my obsession with Robert Schuller and his ministry. My mother said the ornaments were pretty when I hung them on our tree, and my dad agreed that having a positive attitude was important.

While the '80s and '90s brought forth great scandals for televangelists, I was not scarred by such events. The Bakkers faced their share of issues, but while they were my friends at age four, the older me found their style a little too...zealous. I must admit even as an adult that I was sad for Dr. Schuller and his family when in 2010 the Crystal Cathedral, a church I'd watch him build, had to be sold to the Catholic diocese to escape bankruptcy. His reign was over and it stung a bit. As we watch others climb to fame, we always think about how hard it must have been to rise to the top. We never consider how difficult it must be to stay there.

But back to me…Growing up, I never gave much thought to why I was the only kid around watching televangelists while others watched *The Flintstones*, *Scooby Doo* or *The Jetsons*. While I never shared much about my viewing habits with others, I did not consider myself odd or weird or obviously massively insecure. I just enjoyed the shows.

But now, as an adult and a mother, I think about it often. I look back at the kind of child I was, remember my crazy teen years, consider who I am now, and think: wow, I really struggled to believe in myself. Why? Perhaps I am really different. Perhaps I am prone to anxiety. Borderline neurotic even. But what did my parents think?

As a mother myself, I believe I might be concerned if my child was reading religious self-help books at the age of twelve. I might want to even bring up a conversation about it. But this was not my parents' way, at least not in this case. Perhaps they felt Dr. Schuller's message was harmless. They could have been focused on bigger issues, like getting the mortgage paid and managing a busy family life. Maybe they didn't really think about it at all. This was the

1970s, a time when parents certainly didn't over-parent or obsess over their kids' well being the way they often do now.

What I do know is this: My parents loved me. My parents were very laid back. They didn't worry too much about my televangelist viewing habits. Looking back, I can take a guess at the driving factor behind my behavior. I was (am): Curious. Searching. Analyzing. Afraid. I've always been interested in this thing called faith. From a very young age, I've found myself chasing it. I've wanted to find it, feel it, understand what it is all about. I would ultimately spend years in the chase. I would observe those with a strong faith, seek understanding about how it looks, feels and works. But when I was four, I did what I could. I found the beginnings of my faith not from church, not from my parents, but from a 19-inch black box in a cold, musty basement.

DISCUSSION QUESTIONS

Finding God in a 19-inch Black Box

This is a story about a young girl's initial exposure to religion and finding the faith and reassurance she needed by watching televangelists.

What was your first experience or exposure to religion?

Do you remember a particular moment when God became real to you?

Have you ever watched a televangelist's show? What was your reaction?

Many, but not all, televangelists have had their share of legal issues or illicit affairs. In what ways has televangelism affected Protestant religious culture?

In this essay, as a young child, the author found the reassurance she needed through the words of televangelists. Think back to your own childhood. Who did you turn to for reassurance?

How has parenting changed over the generations? Is your own parenting style similar or different from the way you were raised?

Are You A Christian?

We were standing in line, me in a panic, Mary in front of me on her tip toes, and looking over the shoulders of those in front of us, in order to read the list. That Friday would be Field Day at Brookside Elementary School, 1974. It was time to sign up for an event.

"What about the sack race?" she asked, her blue eyes shining as she scanned the list of events.

"Uh, well, okay. I guess we could do that," I responded.

Once we finally made it to the front of the line, Mary printed both our names on the sign-up sheet, making it official. She then tossed her head back and laughed, "It'll be so much fun!"

Fun? I did not see fun in my future. I knew, between the two of us, with our lack of athletic prowess, Mary and I had literally no chance of winning the race. Even the second graders were likely to beat us. And I was right.

We weren't halfway down the field when Mary tripped, causing both of us to tumble to the ground, the ringlets in Mary's ponytails swaying all the way. Lying in the grass, I looked over at my friend in horror. Perfect Mary no longer looked perfect. Her white shorts were covered in grass stains. One of the matching ribbons in her hair had come undone. Her face was smudged with dirt.

We'd lost the race, come in dead last. What now? Picking herself up off the ground, Mary smiled as she held out her hand to help me up. "That was great," she exclaimed as she laughed. "We need to do that again next year!" Despite myself, I smiled back at her. Oh, if I could only be like Mary; it would mean I had made it. If I were as sure of myself as she was, just maybe I wouldn't worry so much about what others thought of me. Maybe I would actually be able to *enjoy* field day.

I'm fairly certain every young girl grew up with someone like my childhood friend Mary. You know the girl I'm talking about. She's the one who wore perfect red and black gingham plaid dresses, complete with Peter Pan collars and black patent leather shoes. Her bright blue eyes danced when she spoke; her smile revealed perfectly straight, white teeth. Her shiny hair fell down her back like a velvet curtain. The boys loved her, and the girls wanted to be her.

For me, that girl was Mary Harrison. Though I'd seen her on the playground before, we didn't officially meet until third grade. Just one look and I knew: Mary was everything I wanted to be, inside and out. It wasn't just that she was pretty or well dressed. There was something about Mary; she exuded warmth, love and acceptance. When I was with her, I could relax into the moment, forget my third-grade fears about dropping my tray in the lunch room, being the last one picked for dodge ball or losing the sack race. I loved her. Everyone did. We were friends for only a short time—three, maybe four years. But because of who she was, because of my experiences with her, my life has been forever changed.

Our friendship began when we both landed in Mrs. Leonard's third grade classroom. We were fast friends, friends who ate lunch together daily, stayed up all night at slumber parties, and shared the most intimate of secrets. And by secrets I mean we told each other which boy we thought was the cutest and what we really wanted to be when we grew up. For Mary this was to be a mom; for me, it was to be a horse trainer. It was during this time in our friendship when I discovered Mary's home life and mine could not be more different:

- Mary had five brothers and sisters, compared to my one brother.
- Mary's mother stayed home and made sure all six children drank their milk. My mother taught college, smoked cigarettes and always had a book in her hand (I never drank milk).
- Mary lived in a teeny tiny house with one bathroom. I lived in a nicely sized '60s-style ranch home, where my brother and I shared a private bath and fought continuously.
- Mary was Catholic, while my family didn't attend church. There was a time when we did, but my brother fought going, and my mother, tired of the fight, gave up trying. Sundays were spent at home or visiting my grandfather in the nursing home.
- Mary's family hung out together and even went on outings. My family didn't do

a whole lot together. Occasionally mother
dragged my brother and me to the
art museum with her, where we'd in-
evitably end up arguing, causing mom to
yell and the trip to be cut short.

In essence, I envied Mary's boisterous home life.
Her home was a home where you could return from
a rotten day and feel safe. My home had two parents
who I thought loved and accepted me. Still, I didn't
feel secure. At the time, my parents were in a rough
spot in their marriage. I could walk in at any given
moment to find a battlefield with two angry adults
lashing out at each other. If they weren't fighting,
they were so wrapped up in their own troubles they
didn't have time for mine. I now know I was luckier
than most: my family's troubles weren't so extraordinary, and they were temporary. My brother Kent
and I were loved, and my parents ultimately did their
best. I just happened to be a timid girl in search of
stability at a time when my family couldn't give it.

Despite being different girls from different stock,
Mary and I became close friends. I was drawn to her
kind heart and positive attitude. The fact that our
families were different did not seem to faze her; she
accepted me for me. She did not seem to notice or
care that I had a bad haircut and mismatched clothes
and was terrible in gym class. I'm sure she never knew
how much I idolized her and her family.

I loved not only how Mary treated me, but her
confident, easy way of dealing with life. Even when
she lost the sack race, even when she was covered

in grass stains and mud, even when she embarrassed herself in public, Mary handled the situation and all her life with grace. If only I could do that, too.

But the truth was, I was nothing like Mary. My teeth were crooked, my hair was a mousy brown, and I had a weak eye and constant eye infections. In addition, my fashion sense (think: Sears brand polyester dress, dingy tube socks, tennis shoes with a hole in the toe and definitely no hair bows) hadn't quite yet kicked in. While Mary slept peacefully, I stayed up nights worrying about surviving gym class and trying to figure out how to make my ponytails look like hers.

But as seemingly perfect and beautiful as Mary was, she too had faults. Because we were close, I happened to know her biggest secret: she struggled with schoolwork. Try as she might in math, science and social studies, these subjects did not come naturally for her. She worked hard, though, and her older brothers and sisters often helped her study, and with that, she managed to get decent grades. I on the other hand rarely studied; good grades came with little effort. It was the one up I had on the girl. But I really never viewed it that way; ours was a friendship based on love and encouragement.

Mary, in her own sweet way, would always compliment me whenever I made an effort to look nice. She'd admire my outfit, never pointing out that striped pants with a Holly Hobby t-shirt and dirty Keds tennis shoes did not make for a good look. In turn, I would ease her worries about passing the times table tests and writing our state book reports, quizzing her at recess. So when Mary asked the question, a question I would seek the answer to for years to come, a question that ultimately turned out to define me, even then I knew her intention was not to embarrass me.

We were washing our nine-year-old hands in the tiny bathroom of our elementary school when in the most nonchalant of ways, she asked, "Are you a Christian?"

Staring down at the faucet, I did not answer; instead I simply continued to wash my hands in the porcelain sink. The question made me anxious. How was I supposed to answer that? *Am I a Christian? What does it mean; is it a kind of religion, like Catholic? Is it bad if I'm not? How can I be in third grade and not know what this means?*

Out of the corner of my eye, I could see her: perfect hair held back with a sparkly gold headband, her velvet black jumper with gold trim. She too was focused on washing her hands. God, Jesus and Christianity were never discussed in my home. I'd watched plenty of Jim and Tammy on TV, but still didn't really understand what made a person a Christian. I had no idea how to answer, but somehow I desperately felt I *should* know.

All I could focus on at that moment were the smells of the elementary school, a mixture of dirt and mustiness, faucet water laced with the acrid smell of sulfur, the scent of cafeteria food lingering in the background. Time was running out; I needed to say something. Quickly, I blurted out my answer. "I don't really know."

Mary turned her head and looked up at me. Her blue eyes reflected kindness. She broke into her same old grin and said, "Well, I am!"

And with that, she grabbed a paper towel from the dispenser and began to dry her hands. That's how things go when you are nine. A question is simply a question. It has no judgment attached to it. It does not reflect on how one will feel about her friend in the future. It's *just* a question.

Hands clean and conversation complete, we left the bathroom holding hands. For Mary the conversation was over, but I could never forget it. I wanted desperately to understand the answer, not just for myself, but also for the girl whose approval I continually sought. We made our way down the hall until we found our place in the girls' line, adjacent to the boys' line. When our class was ready, the two lines followed Mrs. Leonard into the lunchroom. Here we each grabbed our melamine lunch trays, complete with a rectangular pizza, canned peaches, overcooked corn and a carton of milk.

Like our conversation, lunch came and went, but I could not let go of my friend's question. Surely I was a Christian, wasn't I? I knew it had something to do with religion, but that was about all I knew. While my family didn't go to church now, we used to, when I was little. Did that count? And what about everyone else? Were they Christian? Did they go to church? Most importantly, did I look like a Christian? Or did my ignorance show?

If it meant being like Mary, then I definitely wanted to be a Christian. Mary Harrison exemplified everything I wanted to be. Not just for her thick brown hair, bright blue eyes and perfect olive complexion. Not for her sweet, vivacious personality. Yes, Mary was beautiful, kind, popular. But she also radiated warmth and a sense of self I did not possess. And there was something else about her, something I wanted. It would take me years to pinpoint exactly what that was: the love and peace of a devoted believer.

That night, I decided I needed answers. Per our nightly routine, once I was settled in my bed, I'd yell to my mother to come say goodnight. My mother walked over to the door of my room, smiled at me and told me goodnight. She then turned around to turn out the light, and just as she'd reached for it, just as she raised her hand to the switch, I stopped her in her tracks.

"Mom, am I a Christian?"

She turned back around to look at me, the surprise apparent upon her face, and said, "Well, that depends. You tell me."

My mother then walked over to my bed and sat down. And just like the teacher she was, she gave me a textbook explanation of Christianity. She told me anyone who believed Jesus was the son of God was a Christian. She explained that Christians believe Jesus died on the cross to give us eternal life. This was not what I expected. The story felt fuzzy, unreal, like a strange bedtime story. This seemed kind of simple. So all one had to do was to believe in Jesus Christ? Well, earlier I had called on Jesus. That should count.

"Are you a Christian?" I asked pensively.

No matter how much I wanted her to do so at the time, my mother was not going to tell me what to believe. I would later learn that she kept much of her thoughts and emotions to herself. And though I was only nine, my mother was forever teaching me to be an independent thinker. So instead she averted the question with a question.

"What about you? Do you believe in Jesus?"

Everything I did know about Jesus was good. I vividly remembered the paintings of him on the walls of our old church, paintings I'd seen just a handful of times when we did go to church. The depictions of a loving man literally reaching his hands out to others were ingrained in my mind. I recalled the Bible I'd been given from that church at such a young age, the note from Mrs. Jones, the director of Sunday School, spelling out that both she and Jesus loved me. I longed to believe those words, wanted to believe them. I'd watched enough televangelists on TV to notice how happy they all were. And of course I'd observed my Catholic friend Mary's family. With these thoughts in mind, choosing to believe came easy. If it was good enough for Mary, it was good enough for me.

"Well, of course!" I told my mother. She smiled at me and said she believed, too. And with that she got up, walked to my door and turned out the light.

The next day, I excitedly raced off the bus, ran to my classroom and put my lunch box away in my desk. I now had the answer to Mary's question and felt it urgent to share with her.

"Mary! Hey, Mary!"

She was sitting at her desk, completing her morning spelling work. Today's ensemble included a navy blue corduroy skirt, with a light blue polyester paisley shirt, blue knee socks and brown Mary Janes. It occurred to me in that moment that Mary rarely wore pants. She glanced up at me, waited for me to speak.

"It turns out I *am* a Christian!" I explained. I could tell from her eyes that she did not remember yesterday's conversation. I grew impatient with her.

"Remember? In the bathroom? You *asked* me, and I didn't know! Well, now I know. I am a Christian."

At this point, others in the class were looking our way. Mary, in her own sweet way, rebounded quickly.

"Okay," she said with a smile. "You're a Christian, just like me."

She then set her pencil down, got up from her desk and walked over to where I was standing.

"Let's ask Mrs. Leonard if we can erase the chalkboard."

That's when I realized: Mary didn't care if I was a Christian. I was her friend. All she wanted to do was eat lunch with me, play on the monkey bars and erase the chalkboard together. But for whatever reason, I felt it important for her to know my declaration.

Elementary school faded into middle school, and I don't remember seeing much of Mary after that. She found her way onto the dance team and joined the school choir, whereas I began hanging out with new friends who were wicked smart and loved Jackson Browne's music. One of them made me my first gin and tonic. Eventually I heard Mary transferred to our local Catholic high school. I've not seen her since. But no matter, the legacy of Mary Harrison lives on in my life.

In all my years of growing up, all I ever wanted to be was a copycat version of Mary. I grew out of wanting to look like and be her, but I never gave up wanting to be as kind and accepting as she was, as graceful as she at losing the sack races of life. I wanted to declare with Mary's confidence and ease that I was a Christian. I wanted to be a loving reflection of Christ. Without either of us knowing it, Mary was a mentor for me. She, along with so many others I've met throughout my life, taught me how to treat others, how to love myself despite my faults, and how to truly be a Christian. Throughout my life I have thought about Mary as I've made my choices. Without her, I think I might have turned out differently.

DISCUSSION QUESTIONS
Are You a Christian?

A budding childhood friendship with a Catholic girl leads the author to gain an understanding of Christianity.

At what age did you realize you were "a Christian"?

Did you go through any formal declaration of your beliefs (First Communion, Confirmation, etc.)?

Do you have any Christian role models? What have you learned from them?

Are you a Christian mentor for anyone in your life?

In what ways can we be a reflection of Christ's love to others?

The author, though only nine at the time, was embarrassed that she did not know what a Christian was. Have you ever felt embarrassed or uncomfortable about what it means to be a Christian?

Born Again, or Not…

The summer after my freshman year in high school, I got saved.

Sort of.

It all started when my good friend Colleen asked me if I wanted to go to summer camp with her and some of the other kids from our high school. A full seven days with my friends? Seven nights *away* from my boring parents and gallivanting through the great outdoors? How could I resist? It was easy to envision: Colleen and I swimming, canoeing and singing corny camp songs around the fire after we'd spent sunny afternoons hiking through the woods, or maybe even horseback riding. It didn't take much convincing. I quickly agreed to go with her.

Campus Life, a high school youth ministry group from our school, sponsored the camp. While I wasn't a tried-and-true member of the group, I *had* been to a couple meetings. In fact, my introduction to Campus Life had come around earlier that year. During the bleak month of February, Colleen and another friend Dee somehow got wind that Campus Life was planning a spring break trip to Florida for its members. If you know anything about Hoosiers, you know whole families of them flocked in those days to the Sunshine State for spring break. Well, most of them. Colleen, Dee's and my families were the exception.

So when my friends discovered *any* student, even one who had *never* participated in Campus Life, was eligible to go on the trip, we promptly made time for the next meeting and signed ourselves up. The Florida expedition was everything a teen girl could ask for: two straight days on a Greyhound bus followed by a six-night stay in a Holiday Inn a mere twenty-minute bus ride away from the beach. Our days were spent lounging in the sunshine, and our evenings were spent praising the Lord with the entire group.

Truth be told, Colleen, Dee and I weren't at all interested in learning about God or getting to know the other kids. We were there for one reason only: the beach. Our penance, sitting through those nightly praise meetings, was well worth it for a week filled with lying in the sun, playing volleyball on the beach and scoping out the hot guys. After that week, the decision to go to Campus Life camp was a no-brainer. At this point in my life I still believed in God, but that was where our relationship ended. All my attention was centered on having fun with my friends. That we were using a religious organization as a means to our fun…well, that just adds to the irony.

School let out, the calendar flipped to June and on a rainy Saturday morning, my mother dropped me off at the designated meeting location for camp, our high school parking lot. I quickly found Colleen along with our mutual friends Kristen and MaryAnn, who'd also hopped on the bus to Florida with us for spring break. (Dee was done with Campus Life after the Florida trip.) After loading our duffels and sleeping bags, we squeezed into a dilapidated old school bus with some forty-odd other sweaty teens and headed for the hills of southern Indiana. A bumpy hour and a half later, we arrived at camp. Just as we pulled up to the entrance, the grey skies let loose a rain that just might have rivaled Noah's flood.

The weather could have been an omen. For seven days and nights, raindrops pelted and dripped endlessly onto our muddy backs. My visions of swimming and canoeing had not included grey skies, mosquitoes or humidity, but alas, that's what we got. In addition, the facilities were a bit run down.

Our cabin was really an aluminum-sided, concrete-floored building containing ten rusty bunk beds with plastic-covered mattresses. Colleen and I shared a bunk bed; she took the bottom bunk, while I, being the smallest, took the top. Occupying the bunk across from us were Kristen and MaryAnn. At 5´9˝ Kristen happened to be much taller than the rest of us. I recall seeing her feet hanging off the end of her bunk each night. Kristen wasn't much of an outdoorsy girl, and her gear showed it: she had a lightweight pink sleeping bag on her bed, complete with pink pillow. Her white Keds rested underneath the bed; little did she know that with the weather, which ranged from drizzle to cloudbursts, they wouldn't be white for long. MaryAnn on the other hand was used to camping. She and Colleen had grown up together and spent many summer nights camping out in each other's backyards. Both their moms were divorced and worked full time, allowing them the freedom to do pretty much what they pleased. As far as camp experience, I was in the middle. I'd spent a couple weeks at Girl Scout camp in my youth so I knew to expect heat and bugs. I just hadn't been prepared for mud and rain.

Our cabin mates were four girls who happened to go to our rival school. Though we were friendly enough, we spent little time talking to them. They seemed all "Christian-like," or holier than thou perhaps. But Colleen, Kristen, MaryAnn and I were a mighty foursome, for this week at least. The cabin windows and door screens were filled with holes, allowing not only the thick, humid air to pass through but also bugs. We spent a good portion of our time pulling the legs off the multitude of daddy longlegs.

With no swimming due to storms and lots of rain, our activities were somewhat limited. We played a lot of games in the large recreation room/dining hall. Colleen and I became aces at euchre (another Hoosier favorite) and learned how to cheat at Crazy Eights. MaryAnn took to reading books in her bunk while Kristen pretty much followed Colleen and me around and whined about the weather. On the afternoons when the rain let up, the four of us did manage to swim and try out the canoes, but the gnats made even canoeing unpleasant. As camp experiences go, this one wasn't one of my more memorable ones. However, the last night of camp will be forever imprinted in my memory.

The rain had dried up that day, and the sun had even presented itself for an hour or so. Everyone's spirits were lifted. After a not-so-bad day of a group kickball tournament followed by a dip in the lake, we all happily lined up in the mess hall for dinner.

"It's spaghetti!" said Colleen cheerily. She was pale and bone thin but ate more than the rest of us combined.

"I don't know about you all," said Kristen, "but I cannot wait to get home and eat real food."

MaryAnn looked down into the pan of congealed noodles. "It's not that bad," she said. "I mean, as far as camp food goes. Plus I'm starved."

The four of us made our way through the line and found a table that would hold all of us. I don't even like spaghetti, but I was so hungry it actually tasted more like real food instead of the rubbery cheese pizza, tasteless, dry hamburgers and boring bologna sandwiches we'd eaten all week. Afterwards, like every evening, we settled into the recreation room for evening praises.

Evening praises were pretty much the same every night. After singing a few songs together, Gary, our leader, would begin his "sermon" for the evening. Gary was a likeable enough fellow. Tall with a large protruding belly, he was the epitome of the harried, middle-aged man. He had thinning gray hair with a comb-over and kind blue-gray eyes. His sagging physique somehow made him more approachable; knowing he too wasn't perfect made it feel like he was someone you could trust. Gary always started our sessions with honest praises, ones he came up with.

"Folks, we've had another great day today. Can I get a hallelujah?"

"Hallelujah," we all repeated in unison.

"I love to hear your voices, love to hear you all giving God the glory! Let's do it again. Can I get a hallelujah?"

"Hallelujah!"

From here, Gary would ask for specific praises and people would shout them out. We'd hear "Thank you God for our PB & Js today!" or "Praise be to God for bug spray!" Kristen praised God for having two pairs of tennis shoes, so she could dry one pair out while she wore the other. Next Gary would give us something to meditate on, something like "God wants all of us, not just part of us" or "Jesus was a man just like us, but God made him perfect. Think of what he can do with you." Mostly I just sat there picking at my nails during meditations. What was I supposed to be doing? I wasn't too fond of this part of Christian camp, but after Florida, I knew it was pretty standard stuff and nothing I paid much attention to, until this last night.

The last night at camp was akin to a revival. The day in the water, the dry weather and bellies rich with pasta made us a pretty amiable group. Gary started our meeting out with praises like always, but instead of following with a meditation, he went into full gospel mode.

"This is it folks! We've had an entire week spent with God the father, God the Protector and now it's time to go home. Tomorrow you'll get on the bus and head back into the sinful world from which you came. What are you going to do when you get there? How are you going to be a soldier for Christ? Folks, the world needs to know how much you love Jesus!

And you, my friend, need his armor of protection around you. Tonight is the night! Let's give it all to God! Can I get an Amen?"

"Amen!" our enthusiastic group shouted back at him. I shouted with them, but truth be told, I wasn't feeling it. Gary's zeal scared me a little. Did he have to yell so loudly? Why did we have to shout Amen? And what was he getting so worked up about anyway? We'd been talking about Jesus all week, for Christ's sake.

"I want to hear it folks! I want to hear you give your life over to Jesus, *right now*! THIS is the time. Stand up, confess your sins and tell Jesus you want to be his forever!"

I wasn't sure what I expected to happen next, but it certainly wasn't what *did* happen next. One by one members of our camp squad got up and did exactly what Gary asked. Standing up, they confessed their sins. They told our group about lying and cheating and drinking and how now they were different, now they wanted Jesus in their life. Now they would go home and stand up for Jesus.

Was this really happening? What was going on? Was I the *only* one who was uncomfortable with all the shouting and crying and giving it up to God? It's not that I didn't believe. I'd believed in God for as long as I could remember. I just did so a bit more... quietly.

Just as I'd convinced myself that these other people were loonies who weren't like me, my friend Colleen stood up. *Colleen?* With tears streaming down her face, Colleen told her own story of sin and salvation. After that, my friend Kristen shot up, and last but not least was MaryAnn. She too stood up and gave her life to the Lord.

It didn't take long to figure out I was one of the only non-saved campers left in the room, and I was feeling the pressure. Was I going to be the *only* one who didn't get up and tell my story? While I liked Gary enough, none of this felt right, none of it felt to me like what God wanted. But Gary didn't miss a beat. "Do we have any others? Boys and girls, giving your life to Jesus is like washing the sin away. Stand up and tell God how much you love him! Give your life to Jesus, and you'll be born anew!"

The pressure was getting to me. Maybe I wasn't giving this being saved thing a chance. Maybe already knowing I believed, knowing I was a child of God (which I'd learned from Mary oh so long ago) wasn't enough. Maybe telling my story was a declaration of my faith. But then panic set in: I don't have a story! Sure, I was a sinner, but aren't we all? Hadn't God already forgiven me? Did I really need to stand up and shout my feelings for God? What was the point of this entire born-again business anyway?

As all these thoughts raced through my mind, I was keenly aware that Gary was waiting on me; he may have even given me a quick glance. The heat flared up to my cheeks. What would people think of me if I didn't stand up? Does standing up when I'm not feeling it make me a worse Christian? The tension in the air was high, not just because of me. It was like a bolt of energy had shot through the room, and I was feeling the pull.

What was I to do? Though I was skeptical, watching my friends pop up and give their lives to Jesus had made me emotional. I could feel the tears burning in the corners of my eyes. And with that, I could take it no more. I stood up and followed the crowd.

"I want to give my heart to Jesus!" I shouted. "I want him to forgive me for all the things I've done! I want to change!" And that was it. I could not think of anything else to say. I did not have a confession.

But with that, I got an Amen.

We all slept like rocks that night, either because we'd found peace in our hearts or because the physical act of crying and shouting had drained us. For Colleen, MaryAnn, Kristen and me, the bus ride home was full of angst. What would we do now? We'd have to tell our friends we were Christians. People might make fun of us. Everything would change.

No more cutting class or cheating. Even cursing was out. And what about listening to AC/DC? Could we do that? Could we do any of it? I valued my faith but couldn't imagine a life different than the one I was currently living. But deep down, what I really worried about was telling my mother. We didn't talk about God much in our house, and I'd heard her criticize others who talked about being born again. What would she think of me? Would she be happy for me?

Somehow I didn't think so. My mother believed in God, but hers was a quiet faith. Because of that I wasn't too sure of the "rules" for a good Christian faith.

The more I sought out faith in my life, the more confusing it all became. Should I keep my faith to myself or share it with the world? What was the purpose of being born again, anyway, and was it required? The closer we got to home, to reality, the more I dreaded telling my parents what had happened at camp. And for good reason—it didn't go well.

We were sitting at the kitchen table, a place where we often sat for our conversations. My mother had made me bacon and eggs for my welcome-home breakfast, and inside I was surely praising God for that, as my mother was a wonderful cook.

"So," I began. "I got saved at camp last week."

Mom, who was washing dishes in the sink, stopped and looked up at me. "What?" she said. I think my words startled her. "What are you talking about?"

Her eyes were like daggers. There was a bit of crazy in her eyes. My father, so intent on his breakfast, was oblivious. He continued to eat his eggs and read the paper. Maybe he just didn't want any part of this conversation.

I looked down at my food. This was hard. "At camp," I said, "we talked about giving our hearts to Jesus, about getting born again. So I did."

My mother sat down at the table with me. In her eyes I saw anger. At what? Me? The Campus Life group? She had no words, but her face told all. She did not approve. We'd been to church those few times when I was very young, and my mother had told me long ago she believed in God and Jesus. Why wasn't she happy about this? With pursed lips, she looked out the window and took a sip of coffee. Her body language told me enough. It was the end of the conversation.

I didn't see or talk to Colleen again until that fall, after school was back in session. We ran into each other at a party, clinked beers, and went on our merry ways. Even after our vehement vows to Gary and all of the Campus Life group, nothing had really changed. We weren't going to give up our sinful behavior. Based on my mother's response, somehow this felt right. She didn't want me to be some sort of Jesus freak anyway.

What I didn't understand then is that God and the institution of religion are very separate things. While God is constant in his message, religions, churches and people all vary in their expressions of faith. And that's okay. At age fourteen, I got saved, but I did so only due to peer pressure. My true saving came when I was a mere child and chose to believe in and chase Jesus. There was no big witness, no memorable moment and no hallelujah afterwards. And there didn't have to be. We can choose to believe with or without pomp and circumstance. God doesn't care how we do it.

As for my mom, it took years for me to understand her reaction. I later came to understand she detested, maybe even feared, religious zealots. When I was in college, she told me the story of attending a religious revival with her aunt and uncle, who were dedicated members in a fundamentalist church. She was able to laugh as she told the story of watching church members speak in tongues, but at age five, it had terrified her. Her disapproval of my being saved surely was related to this early memory. I sometimes wonder how different my road with faith would have been had she been able to express her concerns to me. But then again, who knows if I'd have even listened or understood? It's all too easy to decide things in retrospect, much harder to comprehend God's ultimate path for us: a road filled with ruts, potholes and perhaps even being peer pressured into getting born again.

DISCUSSION QUESTIONS
Born Again, or Not...

Being "saved" at an evangelical camp leads this teen-aged girl to experience confusion instead of conviction.

Have you ever attended a church revival? If so, what was your reaction?

Do you have a story of being born again, like Paul's conversion on the road to Damascus? Did you go through a life experience that brought you to faith?

Have you been judged for expressing your Christian beliefs?

Do you think Christians judge each other for the ways in which we express our faith? Why do you think this is?

Is it right or wrong to declare your faith just because you want to fit in? Does God judge us for such behavior?

What does Jesus really mean when he says, "You must be born again."?

A Higher Calling

We are sitting. I'm on the fireplace hearth. My mother and a pastor sit across the room on the sofa and loveseat. I can't for the life of me understand why a pastor is here in my living room on a random Wednesday at 5:00 p.m., especially since we never go to church. We've long been members, my dad sending checks annually, but that's about as close to God as we ever got.

I've chosen my spot carefully. I'm hoping I am close enough for conversation, yet far enough away to hide my beady red eyes and the scents of my sins. Yet the smells of tobacco and marijuana are strong; I can even smell myself, which I'm assuming is not a good sign. To my credit, I did not expect to walk into this. Never before had a preacher come to visit us in our home. And with both my parents working full time, most of the time I found myself walking into an empty house.

Sitting upright on the loveseat is my mother. Her hands are clasped nervously in her lap. She is smiling at me, but her eyes can't hide her sorrow over my recent behavior. We never discuss the emotional distance between us, but we both know it is there. At the time I thought she didn't care; now I understand she was a mother without a parental how-to handbook, and I an indignant teenager. To her right, on the couch, sits the pastor.

"Tracy," says my mother, "this is Pastor Brooks." Her voice is raspy, like she has a frog in her throat. I can tell she is nervous, as if she too recognizes the awkwardness of the entire situation. She continues, "He's from the church, First Baptist, and came here today because he wanted to meet you. Remember when you asked about getting baptized a while back? Well, Pastor Brooks has finally come to talk to you about it."

A while back was over a year ago.

The good pastor is looking directly at me, a fake smile upon his face. He is tall, thin, with mousy brown hair. Already, I don't like him. He is hunched forward, with his hands slapped together, resting on his knees. His palms face each other, skinny fingers pointing toward me. I can't help but think of the nursery rhyme from my childhood:

Here's the church, here's the steeple, open the door and see all the people.

Oh how I wish there were more people here.

"So, Tracy," he starts, "tell me a bit about yourself and why you'd like to get baptized."

I am frightened, not by the question but about my ability to get my words out correctly. Because I am stoned. *Really* stoned. At seventeen I had just begun to flirt with rebellion. Thus, getting high was a fairly new thing and something I wasn't too good at. To say it made my thinking fuzzy is putting it lightly. And I sure as heck didn't mean to get this stoned.

It had all started with my lousy day at school:

a D on my French test, Scott breaking up with me, Brenda getting on my nerves in physiology. As soon as school let out, I grabbed my friend Missy, and we took off in my car with no destination in mind. It was a beautiful fall day, so we drove mindlessly up and down the hilly roads beyond our neighborhood, smoking cigarettes and blaring AC/DC as loud as we could. It felt good to get away, to forget everything. It felt good to just be.

An hour later or so, we'd decided to stop in and visit Missy's boyfriend, her *older* boyfriend. David was already graduated from high school and was gainfully employed at Mike's Auto Wash. In just six months, he'd become the assistant manager and gotten his own apartment. It happened to be David's day off, and, avid pot smoker that he was, he was in the midst of getting high when we came by. It was that easy to join him.

That's the thing about getting high: you never know in advance how strong the weed is. All I remember is that afterwards I almost fell down David's staircase on our way out.

Now it seems I am paying the price for my sin. My tongue is thick, and I'm stifling giggles, because really, how awkward is this? I am also angry. Pastor Brooks, this moron of a man, is too late. It had been more than a year since I made the decision, gathered up my courage and told my mother I wanted to get baptized. More than a year since my mom called the church to inquire. More than a year of no one calling her back or following up on the request. Things had changed since then.

"Well, you know," I stammer, "I'm 17. A junior now. I go to high school." That's all I can come up with. Does he know? Is my inebriation obvious or am I just paranoid? Does my mom know? Her eyes tell me something—what I don't know. Lord, help me.

"Good, good," he says. "Well, I guess I should start by saying I am sorry. I understand your mother called a while ago to inquire about getting you baptized. I know we didn't respond, but the church has gone through some changes lately. I wasn't even there then. In fact, I just found out about this recently." He pauses for a second, trying to read me. "But of course, we'd love to baptize you."

A while back was over a year ago. Be it good or bad, I'm in a different place now.

Pastor Brooks continues to smile that fake smile and waits for me to say something. His hands remain perched on his knees, with those bony fingers continuing to point at me as if to inflict guilt. I don't trust him. I see the way he sees me: my ripped-up jean jacket, the stench of cigarette smoke, my flippant attitude. I am the lost girl in an ABC After-School Special. He wants to be the one to save me. No way.

I spent my high school years living a double life. I loved God and wanted to further my faith. When I went on the Campus Life Florida trip in my freshman year, it was for the beach, but of course the messages of faith were getting through to me. But Campus Life camp left me feeling a bit confused about what Christianity looked like. At the same time, I was experimenting with rebellion. If I'm truthful, I'll say that acts of rebellion have their own appeal. There is a certain thrill in disregarding the rules and seeing what one can get away with. Partying was a way to ease the pain of high school pressures, family conflict and feelings of inadequacy. And it was fun, until a pastor shows up at your door when you are inebriated. It is ironic (or is it?) that this was the exact moment God used to gather my attention.

I stare back at the pastor. My mother remains quiet. I suddenly realize everyone is waiting for me. I am supposed to say something, but I don't know how to respond. I am angry. Confused. Hurt. If the church doesn't care about me, then who does?

On top of this, I can't even think because I'm stoned. Part of me wants to lash out, but I'm not a lashing-out kind of girl. Another part of me wants to burst out in laughter over the ridiculousness of the situation. And a small part of me wants to give in and forgive this man, whom even in my anger, I consider to be a decent person, because he works for God. Mostly I just want out of this room.

The silence is deafening. Finally, I find words. "Well," I begin, "I don't know if I want to get baptized anymore. But, I will think about it."

With another fake smile, Pastor Brooks says, "Well, we would really love to have you. First Baptist Church is really growing and changing now. And we'll be revamping our youth group." His eyes shift a bit. "We have a new youth minister."

Since we never go to church, I don't know the story behind this youth minister comment, but I can guess from the look on the pastor's face that there is a scandal tied to it. I don't really care what happened. Pastor Brooks lost me a long time ago.

The minister left, my mom took her sorrowful eyes into the kitchen to make dinner and I took refuge in my room. Nothing was ever again said about my getting baptized. Nor did anyone question me about being stoned on a random Wednesday afternoon at 5 p.m.

Feeling the righteous sting of rejection, I stubbornly refused to talk to anyone about it ever again. Inside, I felt very, very forgettable. How could the church do this to me? Why didn't my mother care enough to ever follow up? Even I knew my desire to get baptized was a bit of a cry for help. I didn't really want to be the person I was becoming. Did she not see this? An unsure teenager feeling the stress and strain of high school was seeking a soft place to fall. Getting baptized was my attempt to get on a better path, but the road was closed for so long, I had decided to take another route.

While he never knew it, in an odd way, Pastor Brooks played an important part in my faith walk. He failed in his attempt to connect with me as an angry teen, but because he came to my house when he did, I was forced to evaluate my situation. And God was there. Even in the awkwardness of the situation, even in my confused state, I sensed his sure and steady presence. I felt his love, his encouragement, his warning that getting stoned on a random weekday afternoon was not the path he wanted me on. And if he had to put a pastor in my living room to get my attention, he would. I sensed that if I didn't change, worse things could happen. It was for me, a turning point.

After that, all thoughts of baptism left my radar. I spent the rest of my high school years partying, but also praying. I was not always proud of my behavior, and while the Pastor Brookses of the world may have been judging me, I never felt God's judgment. Instead I felt his grace and protection. He knew my pain, he knew my heart, he knew I was trying to find my way. I wanted him in my life; I needed him in my life. The declaration of baptism no longer seemed important.

Later that year I joined Young Life, a Christian ministry for teens. I still struggled with my fears and insecurities, but it was a step in the right direction. The leaders at Young Life were fun. They were encouraging but not pushy. They were funny and easy to talk to, much more in tune with teenagers than Gary from Campus Life or good old Pastor Brooks.

The summer before my senior year, I went to Windy Gap, a Young Life camp in the Carolina mountains. I can't say it was life changing, but I have fond memories of that week. Spending a week with my peers, observing those with a strong faith, a faith demonstrated in ways that made sense to me, had a positive effect.

I find that in life, God's timing is oh-so-different from ours. My life and actions in high school were not always congruent with Christian beliefs and values, but the seeds of faith were being planted. My small steps in faith became steadier and continued to push me in a better direction.

I've often wondered what would have happened if the church, my parents or even I had acted differently when I asked to get baptized. What if I'd spoken up to let my mom know how much it meant to me? What if she'd taken a minute to follow up with the church? What if the church had called her back immediately? Would getting baptized have kept me from wandering further away from God, or would it not have made a difference? Ultimately I have to believe my wandering was just one step in God's plan. Or maybe I was just a slow learner.

DISCUSSION QUESTIONS
A Higher Calling

This essay tells the story of a rebellious teen having a chance encounter with a minister to discuss baptism and her thoughts about timing of the event.

Do you think the timing of the pastor's visit meaningful or a mere coincidence? Have you ever felt God utilized a circumstance or event in your life to get your attention?

Why do you think the author was skeptical of the pastor? In what ways have you seen the church or pastors fail people?

The author states, "God's timing is oh-so-different from ours." What happens when we try to control the timing of events in our life?

The author writes about the emotional distance she feels with her mother in this essay. What could she or her mother have done to bridge this distance? Have you had the opportunity to revisit a hurtful situation from the past? If so, what happened?

Once the pastor left, the visit is never again discussed. Why do you think this is?

Have you ever felt judged by God for your behavior? If so, how has that affected your faith?

How do our experiences affect our relationship with God? Do life's trials bring us closer to him, or further separate us from him?

PRACTICING WHAT I PREACH

Faltering in Faith

The words sting. That they are mine, scribbled on the page with my own loose script, is unsettling. It's as if I'm reading someone else's journal.

January 2, 1997
Today I am bitter. Never before have I questioned whether there was a God. And now, I'm losing faith. I keep looking for a sign and there isn't one. It's just day after day of trying to cope. Why is this so hard? It is simply the hardest thing I've ever done.

Ouch. Such raw emotion poured out on the page. It hurts my heart to think I ever felt that way. My faith was being stretched for sure, but was I *really* that unhappy?

A lot had happened in my life since my high school confusion over faith, God and the institution of religion. I'd attended college, married and gotten my first job. Life was good and I was happy. While my faith was still important to me, I had little need to reach out to God when things were going so well. But when the babies came, life got more difficult.

I close my eyes, trying to remember those early days of motherhood. I see my young self in those mom jeans from the early '90s, my Hanover College sweatshirt, my shoulder-length hair in desperate need of a cut. The picture is vivid. My eyes reveal a lack of sleep, yet they are dancing with the love I had for my toddler. She was so active, constantly moving, talking, singing or laughing.

Between caring for her and work, I was forever on the run and exhausted, but she was the love of my life. Of her, my husband and I were so proud. I remember fearing for her: How would she cope when my pregnant tummy let loose of this second child? How would I cope when I quit my job to be home with the two of them? Everything would change.

I squeeze my eyes even tighter as if this could help me see more clearly. I'm searching, searching, trying to understand the origin of these words, written just weeks after girl number two was born. But all I can envision is the smile on my face after she arrived; she was an exquisite birthday gift. Holding her in my arms, so tiny, so snuggly, I could feel she wanted nothing more than to be held by me. With my sweet toddler girl snuggled up next to me in that hospital bed and my newborn girl in my arms, all felt right with the world.

I remember being home with them. It's so easy to recall my young mama-self giving my baby a bath, rocking her to sleep and then playing Duplo blocks with my toddler while the baby slept in the infant carrier. Where is the hardship? Where is the young woman who was so lost she questioned her faith? I read ahead to see if I can remember the me I once was:

I pray and pray and pray but I don't understand. I'm beginning to feel like praying isn't even helping. Is he there? Does he hear me? Does he care?

I continue to scour the pages of my journal. So many stories—stories about bringing the baby home, stories about my toddler and her night terrors, stories about driving around at 2 a.m. to get the baby to stop fussing. On these pages I poured out all my worries. Worries about how long it would take for baby to sleep through the night. Worries about my older daughter adjusting to having to share me, for life. I wrote about that night I was up every hour on the hour with one or other child. I chuckle as I read; I *do* remember that night. My toddler woke me up at 5:30 the morning after, and I was honestly uncertain of my ability to make it through the next 14 hours.

My memories of young motherhood are something I hold close to my heart, but it's easy to see why I was struggling. My husband had to work long hours, and I was drenched in a world full of toys, temper tantrums and dirty diapers. There were times I felt lucky to have survived the day. And I am not alone. I don't know a mother that doesn't have her "war" stories: tales she recounts from the most difficult of days. The telling of these stories is a bonding between mothers. We tell them with pride, but only when those days are long gone, only when we can finally shake our heads over how crazy it all once was. Knowing this comforts me, because it makes me realize the words in my journal were written from a limited perspective, a small piece from the mosaic of an entire life. I have so many other memories from when my girls were young.

I often reminisce about the days of tucking my

oldest girl into bed at night, watching her as she stared with rapt attention at the pages of the books we read together. My heart warms when I think about how I loaded both girls into our wagon, taking them to the playground, to the creek that ran through our neighborhood or just around the block to get out in the sunshine. I remember dancing with them in the living room, baking cookies, our trips to the zoo, the children's museum and the local library. I remember how the older two welcomed their baby sister with open arms, playing with her as if she were a doll. When I think back about those days with my girls, all I feel is love. All I remember is happiness. I can't recall these feelings of…hopeless showing up on the pages of my journal.

The demands of motherhood are fierce: it is true. Perhaps, I think now, I hadn't armed myself well for the battle. I was not prepared for how different life would be when I quit my job (no more adult inter-action or lunch breaks). And while my husband was there to help with the children in the evenings and to support me as best he could, our roles were defined: He was the helper and I was the one tending to their daily needs. I had no idea how heavy the responsibil-ity of seeing these girls into adulthood would weigh on my shoulders. I had no idea how dependent I was upon sleep.

I think about this young mother I once was and I feel for her. I consider how different my life is now, not just because my kids are older, but because of my faith. Now I know I was never really alone. God was with me all along. What would God have done differently if I'd come to him with an open and humble heart instead of an angry one?

I'll never know because in those days *I* was different. My faith lay dormant in a tiny corner of my being. It was there but I did nothing to tend to it. I believed in God but did not attend church, prayed rarely, did not talk of my faith with others. Instead, I only sought him out when things got tough, when I wasn't sure I could handle things by myself, when I was...hopeless.

And because I was without hope, I was impatient and not listening. I did not understand why God wouldn't just wave his magic wand and make it all better. Now I know it doesn't work that way.

There is no magic wand to whisk away pain. I can't snap my fingers to heal my child's scraped knee, can't kiss her cheek to take away the hurt she experiences when she doesn't get invited to a party, can't ease her pain when her grandmother leaves this world for the next. And I can only help her if she comes to me, ready and willing to listen to what I already know and she doesn't yet. Even then I don't know what will happen. I can only hope she learns through each experience, and that she understands that like me, she is never alone.

I am grateful, as I continue reading my old journal, to discover that though it took longer than I'd have liked, I eventually found my way. I found it in my heart to continue praying, to continue seeking, instead of giving up on God. I see now these small steps lead to a turning point in my life.

One day I dug out my Bible and began to read it. To this day I love the words I found to comfort me, the words in Isaiah, 40:31, "but those who hope in the Lord will renew their strength. They will soar on wings like eagles." At that moment I took a step to seek a church home, and though it took time, I found one and began attending regularly. It was my first concrete step in affiliating with a church community. We joined the church and I was baptized alongside my two daughters on Palm Sunday of 1997. What a beautiful day that was. Life got better. And while I didn't know it then, these steps in faith allowed me to slowly open up my heart to God even more. When I opened up my heart, God stepped right up and continued to work in my life.

What if I hadn't? Who would I be today? What would my life be like? If nothing else, we know I wouldn't be writing this book. And I believe my life would be less rich, less peaceful and certainly less hopeful than it is now.

DISCUSSION QUESTIONS
Faltering in Faith

The unreliability of memory and the taking of concrete steps in faith is the focus of this essay. Re-reading an old journal, the author is surprised to see that as a young mother she was overwhelmed by her troubles, unsettled in her faith. She reflects on that time and notices how taking small steps toward belief made a huge difference.

Have you experienced a time where you doubted God's existence? If so, how did you get through it?

How can taking a concrete step in faith, such as joining a church, affect our future steps?

What part does free will play in our faith walk?

How do we stand in the way of deepening our relationship with God?

How does our memory fail us? Is accurate remembering of incidents important or does a mellowing process actually benefit us?

Is the ability to forgive important to our capacity to progress in our walk of faith?

Does revisiting old memories or events in our lives help us move forward in our walk of faith?

The Better Christian

I had been a long time coming to the decision to join a church, to commit. It had been difficult to admit that I needed a church in my life. But arriving there, finding the right church to join: this was no easy task. I recall a time in my early twenties when just asking me if I went to church sent me through the roof. Like the time my husband's boss asked. Tim was a good guy, and I enjoyed his wife, Judy. So when they picked us up to take us out to dinner, I was in no way prepared for what would come next.

"So, are you guys Christian?" asked Tim, as he drove us to the restaurant.

There was a definitive pause before I answered. "Yeah, sure; we are."

Tension pulsed up the back of my neck. I knew what the next question would be, and seeing as we were sitting in the back of their car, there was no escaping it.

"Great," said Tim. "Do you have a church home?" Judy turned around and smiled at me.

Ugh. My husband, the silent type, stared straight ahead and said nothing. From even our earliest days of dating, I somehow was the one designated to answer the awkward questions.

"No," I said, "we really don't go to church." I was leading them straight to the bait. Their next question was to ask if we'd like to attend church with them sometime. No way. I didn't know these people that well, and I wasn't about to go to church with them. I politely declined, and they politely veered the conversation in a different direction.

Right or wrong, I was offended by the conversation. "I hate it when people try to save me," I said to my husband later that evening. "I don't *need* saving." After all, I already believed in God, I prayed on occasion, and God and I—we were good, thank you very much.

I found the question insulting. I didn't *want* anyone trying to persuade me to go to church. I didn't *want* to explain why we *didn't* go. And, I certainly didn't like how it made me feel like I was less of a Christian.

Perhaps it even made me feel like less of a person. Is that what they were implying? Were Tim and Judy being condescending? In retrospect, probably not. But my walls were up so high no one could get over them. The anger their questions provoked in me had more to do with my own complex emotions than anything else. Too bad that dinner hadn't happened just two years later. By then, I was in search of a church for our family and would have been more receptive to their invitation.

After my babies, after struggling as a young mother, I wanted to see what this church thing was all about. I wanted to grow my faith, and more importantly I wanted my girls to grow up in a church, something I had longed for as a child. My husband Steve had grown up going to church but wasn't particularly interested in attending now. Even so, he supported me in my journey, and in turn, I respected his preference to golf on Sunday mornings. The first thing I learned: church shopping is not for the weak.

My first difficulty came in knowing what kind of church to join. The church we'd attended now and then when I was small was Baptist, but in truth, the church's reputation for being strict preceded them. I was afraid to start there. Instead I visited a few newer churches, some of them nondenominational, that were full of young families like ours. Yet I found services more contemporary than I was used to. To me, it did not feel like church. So next I found a small Presbyterian church near our home and gave it a shot.

"Welcome!" said the elderly woman in the pew in front of me. She placed my hands in hers and smiled directly into my eyes. "We're so glad you came today."

This church was about the tenth I'd visited in as many months. It was small and quaint, built sometime in the '60s. The vestibule, sanctuary, pews, the faint musty smell in the air—they all told me this was a church that hadn't changed much since its early days. From the looks of it, the congregation hadn't changed either.

As the pastor gave his sermon, I looked around and saw old men in tweed suits, some with blue-haired wives perched next to them. There were very few families, very few children. Did this matter? I thought so. The church in my head, my fantasy church, had lots of young families. And in my vision we befriended them, raising our children together, in the church. My girls would sing in the choir, go to

Sunday school and join the youth group. This church would accept me as is and not judge me for my wayward walk in faith. Was there such a church?

A small part of me appreciated this sweet lady's kindness, her desire to make me feel welcome. But a larger part wished she hadn't spoken to me. I felt awkward, as if I didn't belong and preferred to remain invisible. I may look Christian enough on the outside, but on the inside I felt…different. What would this dedicated Christian woman think of me if she *really* knew me?

What would she think if she knew I'd yelled at my three-year-old for getting toothpaste on my skirt as I was leaving the house?

What would she think if she knew on most Sundays I was too tired or too lazy to go to church?

What would she think if she knew that for most of my life, church was something I thought was for other people? I was fine praying in private, but doing so in a building with others had never been my thing. Would that make me less of a Christian in her eyes? Then I wondered; now I know. In all likelihood she could have related to my feelings.

Church shopping is hard, doubly so if you've never spent much time in church. It is hardest of all when you fear judgment. I assumed those in church were more righteous than I could ever be. Boy, did I ever assume wrong.

It took me two years to join my first church (I went with Methodist). Two years of trying out contemporary churches filled with families singing along with the big screen. Two years of visiting tiny traditional churches with worn hymnals and bouffant-haired organists. Two years to give up the fantasy of a perfect church and instead accept one that while imperfect, felt right.

Now *I'm* the one in the church pew welcoming another. *I'm* the one hoping she will know I'm not judging her, that I don't care about her past, what she has done or what she hasn't. I only hope for her future. I only hope she will let down her guard and let go of her visions of a perfect church. That she will instead persist in her search, find a church she connects with and experience a growth in faith. That she will eventually develop a personal relationship with God.

It took me years, years of attending church, opening up my heart and talking with others to understand: Churches are full of sinners. Sinners just like me. And that truth makes us all welcome.

DISCUSSION QUESTIONS
The Better Christian

The experience of trying to find a church home is explored in this piece.

Have you ever shopped for a church home? What struck you about the experience?

Have you ever invited anyone to worship with you? If so, what was his/her response?

In the chapter "Are You a Christian?" the author is grateful her childhood friend asked if she was a Christian, yet as a young adult she was offended by the same question posed by an acquaintance. Why do you think this is?

Because she had never attended church regularly, the author fears others in church will not accept her. Is this a reflection of the author's personality, or is it a common experience for non-practicing Christians when they visit a church?

Are Christian churchgoers guilty of judging those who do not attend church?

Do some greeters, ushers, act in a too-forward way—or is that just in the perception of the visitor?

Church attendance and membership has continued to decrease over the years. Is there a growing cultural belief that church is not a necessary component of Christianity?

What can Christians do to encourage others to attend church?

Stretching Past Sunday

I stared at the typed words of her email for quite a while. "All you need to bring is your Bible." My Bible. I had two, actually, but neither seemed appropriate. The first was a children's Bible I'd received from a church when I was maybe five. The second was a King James Version, and while the flowery prose was beautiful, it was also confusing. Joining a Bible study was intimidating enough; if we were going to reference the Bible, I needed to be able to understand it.

I was a young thirty-something and had never before done anything church-y beyond going to church on Sunday (and that was a new development). I'd like to say it was my desire to learn more about God that drove me to say yes when my friend invited me to Bible study. But it was not. It was loneliness.

My husband and I had recently moved from the only town I'd ever lived in to Franklin, Tennessee. We couldn't have been more excited about the move. A promotion for my husband meant more money, heading south meant warmer weather, and we'd found a beautiful house in a lovely neighborhood. Everything about it felt like a fresh opportunity for our family. I had adjusted to my now full-time role of Mommy and was ready to face it head on.

Southerners are known for being friendly, and the people of Franklin did not let us down. We were welcomed easily and quickly by neighbors, and Steve's co-workers went out of their way to invite us out so-cially. But within weeks those we'd met went back to their normal lives and ours became much quieter. It's easy to make acquaintances, but much harder to cross the bridge to become friends.

So my days at home with my two and five-year-old daughters quickly became, well, boring. Though I loved being a mother to my girls, one can only play Candyland so many times before yawning with bore-dom. So when my old college friend Trina called to see if I wanted to join her in a Beth Moore study, I was all in. Adult conversation with the added bonus of reconnecting with my friend? It was like winning the lottery. But a Bible study? I was intimidated.

At that time I knew very little about the Bible, and even less about what kind of people went to Bi-ble study. Would they be like me, or would they be different? Would they be judgmental? Church-going Christians had that reputation, at least in Indiana. I had noticed that Tennesseans were a bit more open about their faith. "Have you found a church yet?" was a common question from those we'd met, whereas in Indiana people (at least the people I knew) rarely spoke of their faith outside of church. The question no longer bothered me as it had in my early twenties; with the move, I *was* seeking a new church home. And true to the phrase, we'd noticed there really was a church on (almost) every corner in our town. Still, attending church and speaking openly about my faith was new to me, and I was a bit out of my comfort zone, but at least I was in the right state for it.

Trina, also a transplant from Indiana, was a sorority sister of mine from college. I knew she had a strong faith, and I think I'd even gone to church with her a couple of times. She was raised in a church and was a much more seasoned Christian than I was. I'd spent my entire life as a believer, but had only recently been public about my faith. I was getting more comfortable talking about church on Sunday. Because I didn't grow up going to church, Bible study intimidated me. It felt like something other people did, not the girl who likely couldn't list the Ten Commandments.

I decided a new Bible was a necessity. But buying one didn't come so easy. A trip to our local bookstore taught me there are several versions of the Bible. Who knew? The Living Bible, the International Standard Version, the New American Standard Bible, The Message. Why so many? How are they different? Which one should I get? Deflated, I left the bookstore empty handed. I went back home and fired off a return email to Trina. "I need a new Bible. What kind should I get?"

God bless my friend. She did not judge me (why did I fear this?). Instead she responded by telling me which Bible she used, the New International Version (NIV). Bingo. If it was good enough for my friend, the lifelong churchgoer, it was good enough for me.

Two days later I drove halfway across town and walked alone into the basement of a church in Nashville. The room was hot, packed and teeming with chatty women. Everyone looked so young, so pretty, so together. What was I doing here? After a quick scan of the room, I found Trina and made my way over to her.

"You made it!" Trina exclaimed. We exchanged a quick hug. "Tracy, this is Maureen. She and I attend the same church service and we're in a small group together."

I didn't know what "small group" was; I could only guess. The three of us chatted about my move, how Trina and I met, their church and the weather. Finally Jennifer, our leader, quieted the group so we could begin. While she went over formalities, I took in my surroundings. There must have been forty women there. All were young and full of enthusiasm. None appeared to have children. Oh, well. Trina was still single and without children, too. What did I expect?

Would they accept me? Would they like me? Would I make any friends?

There was a definite energy in the air of that church basement. The women were upbeat, positive; it was…contagious. Though my shyness remained, my fears of being accepted quickly dissipated. I could do this. I could come every week, visit with my only friend in the state of Tennessee, and maybe make a new friend. Oh, yeah, and maybe I'd even learn something.

Week after week we dove into the wise words of Beth Moore (a best-selling author of numerous Bible studies for women). The lessons challenged me, made me think about my faith in a way I never had before. But what I remember most is being fascinated by the strong faith of the women in the study. What was it about them, their positive attitude? Their willingness to speak so freely about God working in their lives?

The way they seemed real instead of putting on a good face like most people I knew? Whatever it was, it was enough to keep me interested. It didn't matter that I was in a different place, that I was married, that I was new to all of this. These wonderful women accepted me, as is.

My friend got really busy at work and missed about half the study. I missed seeing her, but I continued going. I was learning as much from observing these women of faith as I was from the Bible study. Jennifer, the study leader, exuded such openness about her life; how did she do that? Lisa, a girl I met who was just in her twenties, was young but so wise about life; how did she get so mature? Joanna shared about the hardships in her life, but she was always smiling, genuinely happy. I could only think about how bitter I would have been had I been dealt her hand. Everyone so kind, so positive, so sure of their faith. They seemed so…happy. Joyful. Peace-filled. I wanted that. I wanted their happy. What I really wanted was their faith.

Loneliness isn't fun. It can lead to low self-confidence and increased self-deprecation. These traits make it even more difficult to make friends. So when Trina emailed, loneliness motivated me to action. Joining the Bible study didn't change my life, but it was a life-changing event. By taking that one small step, I was later brave enough to take more steps. Steps in life. Steps in faith. It is in the sum of our small steps that we eventually make progress.

The study ended and my loneliness remained. I took another baby step and joined a church in that new town. Next I attended a Christian parenting class. Eventually I was bringing doughnuts to fellowship hour, volunteering with VBS (Vacation Bible School) and was a fill-in for the ladies' Bunco group. Not all of my experiences were positive. It wasn't as if every Christian I met was beaming with happiness. Christians are just people with faith; they vary in personality, intelligence and maturity. Some of them give Christianity a bad name. But as I dove into a world surrounded by Christians, I discovered some Christians have a certain something; a peacefulness, a knowing, a trust that all is well because God is in charge. How did they do that? It had been my question from the beginning, and it still was. I was fascinated.

What was happening to me? Who was I becoming? It was at about this time my best friend from back home, Susie, christened me with a new nickname: The Church Lady.

It was an accurate description, though she was poking fun at the *Saturday Night Live* character from years earlier. None of the activities I was involved in are so unusual. It's just that they were unusual for me. Believe me, no one would have ever called me The Church Lady in college.

Though life definitely got busier, in Tennessee I still felt the absence of intimate relationships. I missed pushing babies in strollers with my friend Marcia back home, how we hashed out the details of our lives as we walked. I missed the marathon-length telephone conversations and lunches out with Susie. I missed taking day trips to visit my grandparents and in-laws and the occasional Saturday evening dinner with my parents. Oh, how I longed to have a close friend nearby, to connect intimately with someone. I wanted a friend I thought of as a sister. A friend whom you could call just to share the funny thing your toddler said. A friend who would drop by and bring chocolate when you were having a lousy day. Acquaintances rarely stop by with chocolate.

Where was God in all of this? Right there with me. I was praying, and he was answering, only not in the ways I expected. I expected to make new friends immediately. I expected my loneliness to dissipate and my life to become so full I'd neglect my friends back home. But I did not get a shiny, new best friend. What I got was a lesson in patience and persistence.

I became The Church Lady because I needed people in my life, and I figured people with a strong faith might be friendly, welcoming to the new girl. And they were. But becoming The Church Lady didn't solve all my problems. I still had bad days where I poured out my heart in my tear-stained journal. I still cried on occasion and clung to the weekly calls from Susie, cherished the letters my friend Rene diligently sent me every month. But God knew what he was doing. Being lonely led me to rely on him, instead of the people in my life. It drew me to pursue a more intimate relationship with him. I would later discover my time in Tennessee was all about setting the stage for who I was to become. And there were some precious happenings during this time.

Steve and I became closer. Together we took the girls to the wonderful sights of Tennessee. We drove the Natchez Trace Parkway, hiked around Fall Creek Falls, visited Music Row, saw Nashville's replica of the Parthenon and enjoyed Franklin's Dickens of Christmas. I eventually became comfortable with a quiet house; no phone ringing, no one stopping by unexpectedly, no weekend plans to speak of. And then one phone call altered everything.

Steve called one afternoon to tell me things were changing within his company. His department and job would soon be eliminated. It was time to look for a new position. Should he look here in Tennessee, or back home in Indiana? Our new, quieter life was growing on me, but I loved my hometown more. Six weeks later we'd sold our house, purchased a new one and were on our way back to Indiana.

I was more than ready to return to my old life. But I soon discovered I wasn't the same person I once was. The tiny seeds of a faith beyond church on Sunday had already taken root in my heart. The experiences I'd had—going to Bible study, becoming involved in my church, talking about my faith with others—had changed me. I was The Church Lady through and through, and it was sincere. There was no going back.

Everything that happened in Tennessee, a state where there really is a church on every corner and in many hearts, gave me a window into what life with a deep faith can do for a person. It can sustain you in hard times. It can bring you strength, joy and peace, even when life is difficult. A life with God may allow me to be lonely at times, but it also provides the understanding that I am never, ever alone.

DISCUSSION QUESTIONS
Stretching Past Sunday

In this chapter the author discovers the benefit of becoming more active in her Christian pursuits, such as Bible study and volunteering with the church. It changes her.

Loneliness drove the author to join a Bible study and become very involved within her church. In what ways did doing this change her? Do you think she would have made these changes if she had not been so lonely?

What happens when we become more public with our faith?

Have you ever felt awkward when joining a new group?

A Bible study is comprised of a variety of personalities drawn together because of their faith. What are the benefits of joining a faith-based group such as a Bible study? Are there any drawbacks?

Does God care about what motivates us to seek him?

In this age of "spirituality," which seems to mean a vague belief in a higher power without "churchiness" or professions of faith, or

joining any faith group, what are the respon-
sibilities of those in churches to draw these
people in to church? Is that even necessary?

Mea Culpa

Down the hall, up the elevator and through the door on the left...I have arrived. Just walking into the doctor's office brings it all back: the knot in my stomach, the sour taste in my mouth, the subconscious radar going off in my head. I find the physical reminders to be worse than my nearly constant thoughts. At least I can will myself to quit thinking about the baby that no longer is, but I cannot shake the visceral response.

After signing in, I look around my obstetrician's waiting room for a place to sit. I am alone, my husband at work, my two daughters at home with a sitter. All around me are pregnant women. Women with big bellies, women with tiny baby bumps, women with children resting in their laps and playing at their feet. It all serves to remind me about this baby, the one who came to be and left before I ever got to meet her. What would she have looked like? How would she have changed our lives? Did she have something wrong with her? Is that why we lost her?

My name is called. I'm shown to a room. I put on my gown and step up onto the stainless steel examination table and wait to be told my fate. Either I'm healthy enough to try to conceive again or I'm not. All sense of time has evaporated; the wait feels like forever.

"Everything looks great," says Gina, my trusted

nurse practitioner. My exam complete, she looks up and smiles. "It could take up to a year for it to happen," she says, "but there's no reason to think it won't." Her words are encouraging, but her eyes reveal her doubt. She has seen too much in her profession.

Science may be modern, but the miracle of birth is still highly misunderstood.

Gina is the one who walked me through my tears and fears the day the blood came. Gina is the one who called me when my regular doctor was not available. Gina was the one to tell me that I was going to miscarry. Her kind words, her patience with me, her caring voice; this complete stranger held me upright in my time of need. I had never met her, and yet now I feel we are linked for life.

"Okay," I say, forcing a smile. "Whatever happens, happens, right?" I have on my brave face, a face I hope reveals that I am strong, faithful and trusting God with the details. Yet my smile is fabricated. Does she see that? Can she see right through me? Does she know I'm a hypocrite?

Me, the Christian woman who was now busy encouraging others to trust God, who was beginning to see her faith as unshakable, isn't really so sure these days. Me, the one who is, whether I admit it or not, angry with God.

My check-up complete, I get dressed and walk back through the waiting room. I wind myself through the maze of mothers and children whose futures are much more certain than mine. Or are they? One can't really ever know another's full story. I leave the doctor's office with the understanding that in two months I can try to get pregnant again. Time is not on my side. I've just turned 36 and it could take months, maybe even a year to get pregnant. The older I am, the less likely I am to get pregnant and the more likely something is to go wrong. It's not about faith; it's a statistical fact.

I get into my car and drive home. I meet my kids at the door, my two happy, healthy girls who have no idea a sibling was ever a possibility. Am I greedy to want another? Am I rolling the dice on our life? I robotically help with homework, make dinner, take out the trash. This I know how to do. But to confront my emotions, my anger with God? This doesn't come so easily. Instead I bury my feelings. I shove them down deep within the crevices of my subconscious. Alas, my thoughts, they are incorrigible. They continue to spring up into my conscious brain.

Can I go through this again? Or is having another baby not part of the plan? Are two children all God thinks I can handle? Is he telling me to stop trying? Why did this happen? What am I missing? Even though my fetus was just weeks old, she was my baby, living in my body. I had plans for her. Plans with hope for a life and a future, plans for her life and mine, together. Why did this happen to me?

It is the next day when the phone rings. It is my good friend Stacy. I love Stacy. "How are you?" she asks.

"I am good. I am coping. The doctor says I can try again soon."

"Oh good! I forgot this week was your doctor appointment. That is great."

We chat about kids, about school, about getting ready for the upcoming holidays. But then there is a lengthy pause.

"What is it...Stacy?"

"Uh..."

"Tell me."

"Uhm...The timing for this is, well, *horrible*. I wasn't going to say anything..."

"Just tell me."

But she doesn't. I already know what she is hiding. "Are you pregnant?"

"Uh, yeah...I am."

"Stacy! That is wonderful! I'm so excited for you. This is awesome news."

"Thank you! I'm so sorry. I know this must hurt. I didn't want to say anything...I'm just...really excited."

"Of course you are! I couldn't be happier for you."

"It will happen for you, too, you know. I know it will."

Will it?

Ironically, just weeks ago Stacy and I had bonded over a shared cup of tea and confessions about our individual miscarriages. Now she is pregnant, and I am not. Once again, I feel alone.

It is naptime; thank God it is finally naptime. Fifteen minutes of reading *Chicka Chicka Boom Boom* and *There was an Old Lady Who Swallowed a Fly* and I will be free. Free to wallow in my miserable, confusing, envious, angry, sad, out-of-control thoughts.

Sleepy eyes can listen no more. I see my daughter drifting and tip-toe out of her room and quietly shut her door. To my bedroom I go. It is my only sanctuary within this entire three-bedroom, two-bath ranch home. I shut the blinds and soak up the semi-darkness. The lump in my throat formulates before I even hit the bed.

First there are just tears, streaming slowly down my cheeks. But then it is full-out crying. Sobbing, heaving, moaning, shuttering, shriveling. I wasn't crying because Stacy was pregnant. While I was envious, I was at the same time genuinely happy for her. It was just more than I could take, the news that broke the dam. I was crying out of loss: the loss of my baby, the loss of my hope, the loss of feeling God's presence in my life.

We'd grown so close, my Father and me, and then this happened. And when it did, I was hurt. Confused. Sad. I didn't know what to do with my emotions. I had tried praying, had tried to trust him, trust that this was for the best, but I didn't *feel* it. My prayers, my words to God, they were fake.

Finally, I reach a point of numbness. No more "strong girl," no more "things happen for a reason," no more brave Christian smile plastered on my face. No more. The anger I'd been burying rises up within me. Why, why, why did this happen to me?

"I don't get it, God," I whisper aloud. "I just don't get why this happened! I *prayed* about this. I *asked* you to lead me. I wanted this baby so badly. I thought you were on board with this." In my anger and confusion, I confronted (accused?) the God I had always trusted.

"I am a *good* person," I say, "and I am *trying*. Trying to be faithful to you, but I don't *feel* you. Where are you? I feel all alone in this!" I already know my thoughts are irrational: being a Christian doesn't guarantee one an easy life. But still, why did this happen? Why do I feel so alone? Where is God in all of this? I've prayed and prayed and prayed and come up empty. Alone. I feel nothing. The anger continues to well up within me. And then I say, "Where have you been while I've been over here falling apart?"

I immediately feel the warmth envelop me; it begins in my sternum and rises up, warming even my cheeks. Like a balloon deflating, I feel the release of all the pressure in my shoulders, the rush of peace covering me like a warm blanket. And then these words enter my heart and brain:

"*I have been here the whole time. I have been waiting on you.*"

Waiting? For *me*? A flutter in my heart as I realize: this is *not* my subconscious; these words are not from my brain. They are God's words. They are not audible, but they are real. There is no denying it. If I were considering how God might answer me, I'd think fluffy words, something like, "My child, you do not understand, but I have plans for you." I am also confused. What did he mean?

Suddenly the warmth is gone, but the calm remains. The words of Isaiah 41:10 come to me: "Fear not, for I am with you; be not dismayed, for I am your God." I understand now that it is going to be okay. I will be okay. God *is* there. There is no anger over my questioning, no harshness in his words. I am left with only a loving gentleness, all of it designed to help me, not hurt me.

I am a pile of sadness lying in the warmth of my quilted comforter. The sun shining through the blinds brings me back to reality. *Was that really God? What does he mean? What do I do now?* I consider the last few weeks, my pain in losing this baby, my confusion over why and what it meant, my apprehension in telling anyone what happened. And I discover that when I consider these words I've been given, they are true.

I am the one who walked away from God.

Let me repeat this: I am the one who walked away from God. I hadn't even realized it.

I wanted to believe God had better plans for me. I knew intellectually something may have been wrong with the baby, hence the reason she quit thriving. I continued to pray after the miscarriage, but was my heart in it? Was I really trusting God was there, that he would take care of me? No. I doubted him. Doubted his presence. I was angry. I felt betrayed. And instead of praying about these feelings, I'd hid them. But there's no hiding from God. He sees how we act, he hears how we think, he knows our hearts.

But the God I've come to know doesn't judge. He doesn't get angry with me when I pout or question or walk away. When I think I know better than he. And he never leaves me. Instead he waits and waits and waits for me to come to him. Waits until I am ready and willing, because it is only when I humble myself that I can share my full heart with him. It is always a choice to walk with or without; only I can make the choice. He will not make it for me.

As I've continued in my many-stage journey to faith, I've learned God wants all of me, not part of me. There's no sense in my burying my head in the sand over my sins and faults, because he sees them anyway. No sense in trying to rationalize or hide my not-so-great choices, because he already knows where my heart is, and it's not always in a great place. So I've learned to just come clean, to admit my weaknesses. To tell him when I am angry, to tell him when I can't seem to forgive, to ask for help when dealing with my stupid human emotions that show up at the door uninvited. And when I do, I find he often whispers words of understanding to my heart. Words of healing, words that help me. I have to listen hard or I miss them.

I wish I could say that was the end of it, that after God "spoke" to me, I never ever doubted him again, never felt confused by the events in my life, never walked away. But it wouldn't be true. I am as human as anyone: I am not God. I was created to fail and sin, but at least now when I walk away, it's not long before I come running back to the God who is waiting on me. I am learning to trust him not just in good times, but also in bad. When we can do this, God can do even more to increase our faith. And God did bless me with another child, just ten months later: a beautiful, healthy baby girl to complete our family.

DISCUSSION QUESTIONS
Mea Culpa

Anger can harden our hearts. In this story the author discovers she is angry and hiding from God after a traumatic incident in her life.

Faith does not come without hardship. Have you ever doubted God's presence in your life? Have you ever been angry with God?

What can we say to help those who are angry with God for events in their lives?

Many Christians have periods in life when their faith waivers. How can we maintain our faith in God when we do not feel his presence or love?

Have you ever felt God was speaking to you or trying to give you a message in some way?

Sometimes the things we want come first to others. We are envying. What can we do to spot this trait and keep envy at bay when this happens? Why was this state of mind felt so strongly by the ancients, by God, that it was listed as one of the Ten Commandments? Does it seem as serious as the others?

Forgiveness does not come easy for many of us. How does God change our hearts when we are harboring negative emotions?

Follow(ing) the Leader

Sometimes we choose our path in life, and sometimes the path meets us where we are and offers up a new route. I never planned to befriend the dying, to become a hospice volunteer. No, the decision was never self-motivated; I did it because I'd felt a nudge from God.

It was an ordinary day, and I was at the library with my three daughters. I was trying hard to get them out the door, but my oldest was dawdling, glued to the library's display window.

"Sarah," I said, "come on, we have to get home. Mommy has to get dinner going."

"Look, Mommy, they are having an American Girl tea party!" Between the kids, my part-time job, two dogs, a hamster and life itself, there was no time for tea parties. I walked over to my daughter and gently placed my hand in hers. "Yes, I see, now come on." It was then that I saw the poster asking for hospice volunteers.

Hospice? For some reason that word caught my interest. I knew little about hospice care, beyond the fact that if you were on it, you weren't long for this world. For a moment I stared at the poster. The words penetrated deep into my brain. It would be awful to be on hospice, to just know the end is near. Who would ever want to volunteer to work with the dying?

What about you?

Just like that, the thought came. If it were just a thought, I'd have ignored it. But unfortunately with it came a feeling. Call it what you will: a knowing, a sudden realization, a strong understanding that this was something I needed to do. I ignored the feeling and instead went to the logical side of my brain. What? That's crazy. Where did this idea come from? *Me, a hospice volunteer?!* I know nothing about nursing care or illness or dying. Surely my silly brain was making this into something it was not. With that I left the library, my pile of books and three daughters in tow.

Later that night, as I made dinner, thoughts about volunteering continued to crowd my brain. Why am I still considering this? Am I crazy? I don't have time to take on anything else. And then the ultimate question: could this be God, nudging me? I'd heard people say God called them to do things, but I had never experienced such a thing. Nor did I understand how God went about delivering his messages.

What does it mean to be called? People I'd known, those who had a deep faith, had told me their stories, stories of when God spoke to them and sent them in a specific direction in life. Called them to go into ministry. Called them to become a foster parent. Called them to go on a mission trip. But how did it happen? Just how did God speak to them, and most importantly, how did they know it was God? When I asked, these friends would tell me they just knew. *Just knew.* "For many are called but few are chosen," Jesus says. How does that fit into the picture of hearing a call from God?

Hearing God is experiencing a knowing. The idea itself invites skepticism. How does a person differentiate the voice of God from his own? I guess this is why it is called faith. You have to trust the knowing, a feeling or gut reaction to something even when it isn't based in logic. It's a choice, choosing to believe in the visceral understanding that what you're experiencing is not from your own mind.

For me, becoming a hospice volunteer was a big step in trusting my faith. It started with this knowing, this pervasive thought, one that wouldn't go away. But as a writer, I must be careful; I *do* have an active imagination. I didn't want to get carried away with my thoughts and emotions. But the notion of volunteering persisted. So next I took a baby step. I called to get more information.

Connie, the volunteer coordinator for the hospice organization, was easy to talk to and answered my questions cheerily and without pressure. There was no experience necessary, and I'd be trained by the hospice organization. I would be assigned to one patient at a time and was asked to spend an hour a week with him or her. I needed three references and a TB vaccination before I could start.

My gut was telling me to say yes, but I was afraid. I was famous for over-committing my time. What if this wasn't God's direction? What if I hated it? What if I couldn't handle it? I didn't want to say yes and then back out. I was clearly beginning to understand this was a nudge from God, but my courage had not caught up with me. So I continued to pray, searched scriptures, tried to clear my mind so that I could hear his voice instead of mine. It took me a month to say yes. Yes to God, yes to becoming a hospice volunteer.

My first patient was named Katie. She was 38 years old and bedridden with a terminal illness. I was terrified to meet her. Though I'd gone through training, it was nothing compared to the actual thing. Walking into a complete stranger's home (a dying one, no less) to offer comfort, reassurance or whatever is needed is no small task. Lucky for me, when God asks you to do something, he also supplies you with the means to accomplish it.

I'll never forget my first visit. Katie lived in a tiny one-bedroom apartment just a mile away from my home. Her sister, who cared for her, answered the door. "She's tired," she said, "but excited that you are here." I followed her to the living room of the apartment. And there Katie was, a woman with soft brown curly hair and eyes that shone brightly, sitting propped up in her hospital bed. Waiting, it appeared, for me. Outside of being pale, she did not look sick. But the signs of illness were there; next to the bed sat a small table covered with prescription bottles. Next to that was her walker. On the floor lay a pair of worn pink terrycloth slippers. Thirty-eight years old. One year younger than me. She lived just one mile away, but she was living in a completely different world.

Katie listened eagerly as I told her about myself and my life. I asked about hers, but she'd been sick for so long she no longer worked, had never married and didn't have children. So we went back to me. At first I felt awkward, as if I were bragging about my beautiful life, my three precious children, my *healthy* body. But she was the one asking all the questions; she was the one listening intently to all my answers.

Later I wondered if focusing on my life was a way for Katie to escape her own. After an hour of getting to know each other, we agreed on a time for me to come visit the following week. I gave her a quick hug as I left. Katie seemed excited about our budding friendship, and I was, too. She died two days later.

My second patient passed away before I even met him. In truth, I was relieved. After all, my track record thus far wasn't so good. But before the week was out, my volunteer coordinator assigned me to a new patient: Frank.

Frank and Elsie had been married for over fifty years. A sweeter couple I've never met. They had five children, multiple grandchildren and two very fat cats. Elsie was the caretaker for Frank, who had heart and lung problems. On day one she greeted me at the door with bright blue eyes and a wide smile. Elsie ushered me in and gave me a quick tour of their lovely home. The shining wood floors, bright yellow curtains and orderly kitchen showed me this was a home filled with love. It was also a virtual haven for the many green plants, the cats and her two birds Sam and Sunshine.

After we'd toured her flower gardens, Elsie brought me back inside to meet Frank. A large man with dark eyes and a full head of silver hair, Frank was well over six feet tall to my five. He had little to say to me beyond hello. My job as a volunteer was to keep him company while Elsie went upstairs to sew. I was to make sure he kept his oxygen mask on; he often tried to remove it.

I was again terrified. Could I do this? This terse man outweighed me by well over a hundred pounds. What would we talk about? What if he fell down? What if he wouldn't let me hook him back up to his oxygen? At the heart of my fears was this: what if he (or anyone for that matter) died on my watch? Please, God, you brought me here…

It didn't take long to get Frank talking. I figured out he was a sports fan, so we spent our visits talking sports and playing with the chubby cats. He did disconnect from his oxygen, but I was able to coerce him into hooking himself back up. I genuinely liked Frank, and I think he enjoyed my company. Even the cats liked me.

Visiting Frank and Elsie wasn't so different from visiting my own grandparents. I felt comfortable around Elsie and found myself learning a great deal from her. I saw her respond to Frank with love and patience, even when he was cranky. I watched her light up as she spoke about her grandchildren and saw sadness in her eyes when she occasionally unloaded a bit about the hardships she was dealing with. Yet no matter what, Elsie always framed her circumstances through this lens: she knew God was with her, knew he had plans for her life. Could I ever be as strong in faith as she? I could see the peace it brought her, but could not imagine ever being so strong, so sure of God's love and presence.

Three months later Frank's heart finally gave out.

Was I sad? Yes, but it's a different kind of sad from when a friend or family member dies. I would miss him, but in a way I was happy for him: no more suffering and no more having to take thirty-odd pills every day, and he was finished with that darn oxygen machine. Good riddance. Though Elsie doted on him, caring for Frank was hard on her. It was in many ways, a blessing.

Shortly after the funeral, I called Elsie to see how she was coping. It was then that she told me she'd seen a dove on her porch just after Frank passed. It wasn't the first time either; Elsie had lost two children within the last ten years. As each child passed (one from an overdose, one from a car accident) she'd found a dove perched in her garden right after hearing the news. Elsie's doves gave her peace in knowing her loved ones were okay.

I would miss both Frank and Elsie. I loved her story about the doves, but I wasn't sure I believed it. I had yet to lose anyone close to me, and I chalked her story up as a way to help her feel better about her losses. I decided it didn't matter what I thought; I was glad Elsie gained comfort from her faith. But leave it to God to undo my skepticism.

The very next morning I found my dog barking furiously out our great room window. Molly was older and rarely bothered to bark at anything. Absorbed in my work, I ignored her. But when she wouldn't stop, I finally walked over to the window to see what the ruckus was about. There straight in front of me, perched in our red bud tree, sat a dove. He stared directly at me, and I at him. Our eyes locked for quite a while. What in the world? Yes, doves are common, but I'd never seen one in our yard. And why would my dog bark at a bird in a tree? This couldn't be a coincidence; it was a message. I suddenly felt foolish for not believing Elsie in the first place.

I continued to volunteer for the next three years. There was Charlene, who lived in a ramshackle apartment in the projects with her sister and three daughters. Oldest daughter Jenna, only 16 years of age, could barely take in that she and her sisters would soon be moving in with her aunt. Then there was Dorothy, who loved to talk about her younger years as a competitive swimmer. And Vivian, who never spoke, but one day miraculously sang out loud when I played her favorite CD. There was Robert, whose wacky roommate always wanted to hang out with us, in his underwear. And Jean, a dear homeless woman with no family, no one at all to visit or care that she was leaving this earth, except for me and her nurses.

I prayed for my patients and their families. I brought them ice cream and chocolates. I gave wheelchair rides, massaged shoulders and held hands with those who longed to be touched. Through it all I had learned the importance of being present, the value of life, the gift of one more day.

But now I was struggling. My current patient was Estelle, and she had end-stage dementia. I knew little about her because, like Vivian the singer, Estelle rarely spoke. I'd been told she had a son, but I'd never met him. Many of our patients had the support of their families, but not all. Some had no one left or were simply neglected by their loved ones. I supposed this was the case with Estelle's son.

Estelle mostly spoke gibberish. She was wheelchair bound and no longer able to hold her head up or make eye contact. This made it difficult to connect with her. Sometimes I rubbed her shoulders or massaged lotion into her hands. Often I pushed her around in her wheelchair, chatting to her as we rolled around the nursing home. In the end I spent most of my time counting down the minutes until I could go home.

While I'd always loved my volunteer work, with Estelle I felt useless. Most of my experiences brought the reward of knowing I had brought joy to a person's day. But with Estelle so unresponsive, I couldn't imagine I was doing her any good. Was my time with her a waste?

One day, though, our visit went surprisingly well. I was giving her a ride in the wheelchair and noticed she seemed alert. I asked her a few questions and received logical answers. She told me she'd worked in a factory, had three children and lived on a farm with six dogs. I wasn't sure about the dogs, but suspected at least some of what she told me was true. Our conversation gave me hope, but it didn't last. On our next visit, Estelle was back to staring blankly into space and whispering nonsense.

But this week, Connie had called to let me know Estelle was declining. I knew from experience that when Connie called I had just a day or two to visit. If I wanted to see Estelle, I needed to make time for it, and soon. Should I go visit her? Would it even matter?

I'm embarrassed to say my heart was torn. I typically extended every effort to see my patients one last time before they passed away. But Estelle wasn't even aware of my visits. Part of me wondered, what's the point? My time with her wouldn't make a difference.

In the end I was overcome with guilt. What kind of volunteer blows off her last visit with a patient? Yes, it was raining outside, and yes, I had a million things to do, but this was it. It was my time to say goodbye to Estelle.

An hour later I was in the nursing home where Estelle resided. At least hers was decent. Many of them weren't; the smells of urine, sickness and bland foods like overcooked cabbage often overwhelmed me when I walked in. But Estelle's was a clean and comfortable place. It was a Sunday morning and all was quiet. I was deep in thought when I turned down the hall toward Estelle's room and literally ran into a man headed toward me.

"Oh! I'm so sorry!" I exclaimed. "I wasn't looking where I was going."

His smile told me he was a kind person. "No problem. I was just headed out to get coffee." He paused before adding, "You aren't Tracy, are you?"

Immediately I knew this was Estelle's son. It turned out I was right. How had we never met? I had wrongly assumed Estelle wasn't close with her children, that maybe they never came to see her. I couldn't have been more wrong. Brian came to see his mother every day during his lunch hour, a time when

I was never there.

After getting his coffee, Brian met me in Estelle's room. At first I felt awkward. What exactly does one say to a man who's waiting for his mother to die? For a while we sat together in silence, the only sounds being the hum of the oxygen concentrator and the rain softly pelting the window. I looked up at Estelle. She looked so peaceful, cozy even as she slept, her quilt resting just below her chin. Finally, I mustered my courage. "You know," I said, "a couple weeks back we had a really good visit. Estelle told me about her life and I wonder how much of it was true."

I told Brian all she had shared with me that day, about her life on the farm and in the factory. Brian, who was not much older than I, smiled. "It's all true," he laughed, "except for the dogs. We only had one dog!"

This was a deathbed scene like nothing I could have imagined. We talked a bit more about Estelle and what a wonderful mother she was. He told me he came to see her every day. For our entire conversation Estelle was unconscious, but it felt like she was with us. I began to see Estelle for who she was—not just an elderly woman with dementia, but a person. Estelle: wife, mother, factory worker, daughter of God. I felt ashamed for not wanting to come here today. I felt badly for having judged her son, whom I'd never met.

Brian interrupted my thoughts. "I don't know how much longer she has," he said, "but I am here for her for as long as it takes." He smiled. "I don't mind, and I am ready when she is. This is her life, her journey; she'll go when she's ready." Brian was not crying, was not upset; he was simply, unselfishly there for his mother in the moment. He was waiting for his mother to be ready to go.

An hour later, I left Brian with his mother. I said goodbye to Estelle and walked out. The events of the day rolled around in my brain. Brian came here *every* day. In all this time, I'd never run into him. But today of all days, we met. Could it have been for a reason? And then came the realization, the *knowing:* our meeting was for Estelle. Could it be that as Brian and I spoke together, Estelle heard Brian's voice? They say the last sense to go is hearing, that though it may appear those we care about are beyond our reach, unconscious, they can instead be listening to us. Did she need to hear him say out loud that he loved her, that he was okay with her leaving him? Did his voice affirm all she needed to know before she could let go? I felt certain God had given Estelle the answers she needed so she could leave this world in peace.

Connie called me two hours later; Estelle had passed away in her sleep. I wasn't at all sad. In fact, I felt happy. Happy for Estelle to be released from her crippled body and mind. Happy to know Brian was at peace with his mother's passing. Happy to have witnessed God in action that morning.

My faith grew exponentially during the time I was a hospice volunteer. By saying yes to this first nudge, I learned how to follow God's lead. With practice I grew to know more about deciphering his "voice" from my own. I became convinced that no matter how odd or scary the suggestion, God has the details handled if I will just be brave enough to follow. To this day, I sometimes struggle to answer his calls; logic and human nature often pull me away. But I've also learned the more I trust, the more he speaks to me. And his ways are always better than mine.

My compassion and understanding for people also grew. One can't work with the dying and not gain a perspective on the value of life. Hardship is real and it does not discriminate. And while we can't solve the problems of those we love, can't take away their troubles or save them from terminal illness, we can love them through it. We needn't feel awkward; our family or friends already know where they are headed. We can pray for them. We can be present with them. We can sit and wait patiently until the individual is ready to go. It is important to do that, and though it may not feel like it, that stillness, companioning and acceptance are enough.

All of this happened, all these experiences and learned lessons came simply because I said yes: yes to one small nudge from God. Who would I be now if I had listened to logic, ignored the call, went on with my busy life? I don't know, but I do know I'd be less. When I say yes to his nudges, when I pay attention to the knowing, God can use me to bless others. And when I do, it is I who feels blessed.

DISCUSSION QUESTIONS
Follow(ing) the Leader

This essay explores what happens when we answer the call to serve and shift our priorities. It also challenges us to ask ourselvs whether there are spiritual occurences in this world beyond our understanding.

Have you ever felt encouraged by God to go in a certain direction? If so, how did you respond?

What do we miss out on when we ignore God's call?

How important is service in your (busy) life?

The author assumed the worst about Estelle's son. How can we refrain from jumping to conclusions about people we do not know?

Have you ever felt like God worked through you for another? If so, how did it make you feel?

Do you believe it is possible that we are given signs from our loved ones who've passed away (like Elsie's doves)? Have you ever experienced such a sign?

In what logic-defying ways does God reveal his presence in our lives? Has God revealed himself to you in an unusual way? Is there another explanation for what happened or are you willing to accept a spiritual answer?

ALTERED FAITH

How Did I Get Here?

I am standing at the room's entrance. Everyone is filing in, one by one, to greet me. Family and friends are everywhere, surrounding me, yet in the midst of all the chaos, he finds me. Pastor Ray immediately envelops me in a hug; his rather large frame encompasses my small one. I'm not completely comfortable, being that I am not a hugging sort of person. Even as this is the pastor of my church, I'm in such a state of distress and uncomfortable with the physical hug. Even so, I readily accept his embrace. I am grateful he came.

He stands back, places his hands down upon my shoulders and looks directly at me. His concern is reflected in his eyes, his empathy revealed. This just adds to my anxiety, makes me want to run and hide, because who wants to be at her mother's funeral, seeing hundreds of people feeling badly for you? It all just makes me feel worse. And besides, I'll be fine; I always am. I know how to be fine.

"I'm so sorry, Tracy," he says. "How are you holding up?"

"I'm okay," I answer. "Obviously it's hard, but we are all hanging in there."

"And your Dad...is he here?"

I feel the tears welling in the corners of my eyes. "Yes, he's over there, standing next to Steve and the girls." I look over to see my husband Steve lovingly place his hand on my youngest daughter's shoulder as he chats with my father. "I'm so glad Dad was able to come."

"And your brother...he is doing all right?"

I don't really know how to answer this question. My brother has lingering symptoms, but I'm hopeful. "He is still on the mend, but I think he's going to be okay." I pause before adding, "He is so lucky."

These are the questions, the three questions I have been asked repeatedly in the last two weeks. Because in that time, my mother has died, my brother has had a stroke followed by emergency surgery, and my father, who has Parkinson's, has forgotten to take his medications, and he too, wound up in the hospital. All this in *two* weeks. I should be falling apart. Twenty years ago, I would have.

But here I am, not falling apart. I'm greeting the crowd at my mother's funeral. We're in the mortuary's chapel. It's a large room, with walls covered in gold-and-white striped wallpaper, colors designed to sooth grieving souls. In each corner sits a fake plant on an urn-like pedestal, adding garish color to an otherwise bland room. At the front of the room is a ornate fireplace and in front of it, a table playing host to the urn holding what is left of my mother. Next to it hangs a colorful collage of photos, a leftover from my parents' fiftieth wedding anniversary celebration a couple years back. In the corner sits my laptop playing a slideshow of photos of my mother. My mother: in her youth, graduating from college, holding her babies, skiing in Vermont. It is but a glimpse of a woman who lived a good and full life. In the background, a collection of my mother's favorite hymns plays softly. The irony does not escape me, since my mother hardly ever attended church.

There are at least a hundred people milling about the room. I've spent the last thirty minutes greeting the line of visitors as they came in to pay their respects. The tears won't stop releasing themselves from my eyes as each person I speak with tells me how they knew my mother and how she touched their lives. It's a shock to my system to hear these stories. To think of her as a teacher, a cousin, a friend. Was she really like these memories of her? I never knew. My vision of my mother is flawed; I saw her *only* as a mother. This was just one part of who she was. I consider: Did I know her at all? Such thoughts are overwhelming, yet knowing what she meant to others is oddly comforting.

I am sad, relieved, hating this day but in some ways, glad for its arrival. Between my father's hospitalization and my brother's recovery, it's been two full weeks since Mom's actual passing. Waiting for the funeral has been torturous, and I will be glad to put it behind me.

Chatting with my pastor, I am about to discover a facet about myself I never knew, even after all these years of growing in my faith.

"Are you *prepared* for the service?" he asks gently.

Prepared? What does he mean? Am I prepared once again to test my faith?

"Yeah, the people here have been so helpful, everyone has," I say. "I'm just, well, I'm worried about the eulogy. I wrote it and I want to read it," the lump in my throat resurfaced, "but I don't know if I can."

The eulogy had been difficult to write. How does one sum up a person's life in ten minutes? I didn't even know how to write a eulogy, and when I researched examples of them, they just didn't seem to fit my mother. So instead, I'd done my own thing. I did what I know how to do: I wrote a letter to my mother. In it I told her how much I cared about her and what I would miss most about her. It was emotionally charged. My biggest fear was breaking down and not being able to read it. I wanted to honor my mother, and simply put, I was afraid I'd blow it.

Of the four pastors in our church, Ray, the head pastor, is the one I'm in contact with the least. But he knows my story; *all* the pastors at church know my story. And that isn't all, because at this point in my life, when things get bad, *really bad*, I remember I am not alone. God is here with me. My church is there for me. My family and friends care for me. And I am not afraid to reach out. I can try to weather life alone, or I can reach out, risk vulnerability, allow others to help me. Allow God to help me.

Pastor Ray gently asks, "I'd like to pray with you. Can we pray?"

Without hesitation I answer, "Yes. Yes, I'm ready."

Faith is a funny thing. At it's very crux we're asked to believe in what we cannot see. It can be hard for even the most faithful among us. So while I believe God is in control, it doesn't mean I am not afraid.

I need my pastor's prayers; I need the reminder of God's promise: that he is there with me, his hands are holding me up, his strength helping me keep it all together.

So right there, right in the middle of more than a hundred people and the buzz of conversation and background music, I allow Pastor Ray to take my hands. Together we close our eyes, and he asks God to watch over me, to give me the strength to read my mother's eulogy, to give my family peace and love.

It's not something I'd have done twenty years ago. Twenty years ago public displays of faith embarrassed me, felt foolish to me even. I would never have risked looking foolish or allowing the world to know I was a Christian. I may have believed, I may have talked with those closest to me about my faith, but I would never have prayed in public, would never have reached out to ask others to pray for me. I believed, but my faith was private, quiet, personal. Like my mother, you'd have only been able to tell I was a believer by the soft hymns playing in the background of my life.

But throughout the years, through trial and error, I have grown. I have changed. Somewhere along the line I shed the fear of allowing others to see what I believe.

When I started my journey in faith, I never knew where I'd end up. I never pictured who I would become or what my life would be like. I just kept putting one foot in front of the other. With baby steps, I explored religions. Joined a church. Got baptized. Joined a Bible study. Journaled. Prayed, failed and learned. And, finally, trusted. All these little changes led to big changes, and now, I am someone different. A strong believer, one who is not afraid to express her faith both privately and publicly.

I'm still the same me I've always been: I struggle with confidence, fret over stupid stuff, get frustrated with traffic and politics and my family members. I still sometimes struggle to trust in what I cannot see. But I *believe*. I have felt God's presence, have seen him in others, have experienced him whispering words into my heart. I am happy in my faith. I no longer worry what others think about it.

When Ray prays with me, the world around me disappears. I can physically feel the profound stillness enter my body. It spreads from head to toe and calms me. It's a somewhat familiar feeling, as I have felt it before, though not *every* time I pray. Even as I pray daily, I sometimes have trouble letting go and giving it all to God. I don't always want to humble myself before him. But when I am able to do so, when my prayers are raw, deep and straight from my heart, then I feel it. God's power, love, warmth.

And today with Ray's prayers, I'm really ready to let go and trust. I need my faith family.

Everyone is seated. The service begins. It is both heartbreaking and beautiful. And finally it is time. With a deep breath and a tiny lump in my throat, I read my mother's eulogy.

A Letter to My Mother

by Tracy Line: March 28, 2014

Dear Mom,

I'm sitting at my desk, and I'm trying. Trying to calm my thoughts, trying to ignore my anxiety and trying to write a eulogy for you, the most important woman in my life. And I can't seem to do it.

My thoughts, they are jumbled. My doubts are taunting me. And the words, well, the words just aren't coming. Because how in the world does one write a tribute to honor her mother, a tribute that tells the story of a life well lived in a three-minute speech? It feels impossible.

So enough. I give up. I quit. I've closed out the "How to Write a Eulogy" search results on my laptop. I will not read one more sample eulogy from funeralhelper.org. And I'm done watching videos from "8 of the Most Amazing Eulogies of All Time." Instead, I'm giving up on Google, and I will find my words here where I always do: in my heart. I will write them in Microsoft Word and I will do so in a letter to you.

You, Mom, were a good one. You were there for me always, even when I didn't recognize it, notice it or want it. You held me in the hospital when I was weeks old, hoping and praying I would recover from a horrible eye infection and that I wouldn't lose my sight. Well, you got half your wish since I can see out of one eye. But what really matters is that you were there, even when I was too young to remember or understand.

You were also there for me throughout my childhood. You took me to eye appointment after eye appointment until I became strong enough to fight off all those eye infections. You drove me to Girl Scouts and basketball games and art lessons and the orthodontist and to friends' houses for sleepovers. You put up with me when I was a teenager, a time when I was certainly not the nicest person to be around.

You made me get a job. And I mean made. I remember it well. I came down the stairs on the morning of my sixteenth birthday and you said, "Happy Birthday! You're 16 now and that means you can get a job," smiling all the way. I knew it was coming because you did the same thing to Kent three years earlier. It was a subject that was not up for debate in our house. But working taught me so much: how to manage my time, how to get along with others and how to handle my own money.

Another given in our home was going to college. You were a big believer in education, but at the same time you never pushed. Instead you and Dad always encouraged. You taught me to study what I loved and get a job I enjoyed. These lessons made me the independent woman I am today. I believe they have played a huge part in my being able to live a really happy life. And I thank you for it.

The truth is, I will miss you. There are so many things I will miss. Your wonderful meals, always served on a beautiful table complete with a linen tablecloth, candles, china and the most amazing food. Your recipes. I didn't get them all yet. I still don't know how you got your gravy just right, and I don't have your homemade salad dressing recipe. Something tells me Dad doesn't know it.

I will miss traveling with you. Remember Paris? You, Betty and I getting locked in the train on our way to Versailles? And then there was New York. We walked and walked and walked. Our feet hurt so badly we decided to go into a rather suspect Chinese foot massage shop. It was dark and dingy, and as we lay on cots getting our feet rubbed, we held tightly to our purses. But how we laughed afterwards, and we both agreed it was the best foot massage we'd ever had.

Then there was the time after I became a travel agent and asked you to come with me to "inspect" a health spa in Illinois. We had three days and two nights of wonderful meals, tai chi, yoga and swimming and pampered ourselves with massages and pedicures. I remember chuckling because you snuck in wine for us to drink in the evenings. Only you, Mom.

I will also miss Pub Club, the brainchild of Kent, of course. That weekly Cheers-like gathering when you, I, Kent and Dad and whoever we'd brought with us went out for pizza and beer. Forever it was a Tuesday night standard. We had our own fun and also brought joy to the others in the pub. Life's hardships always seemed to dim as we laughed away our troubles each week. I will hold those memories close forever.

But most of all, Mom, I will just miss you. Talking

with you, laughing with you and learning from you. I'll miss our lunches out. I'll miss telling you about the girls and how they're doing. I'll miss laughing every Christmas because you got the tags on the gift bags mixed up. You've taught me so much, Mom, but most of all, you've taught me to be myself, follow my dreams and live life to the fullest. I can't think of any lessons more important.

Thanks be to God; I did not blow it.

DISCUSSION QUESTIONS
How Did I Get Here?

The author seeks comfort in a very public prayer with her pastor at her mother's funeral. She then reflects on how years of practising faith have changed her and made her a stronger person.

Have you ever prayed in public? If so, did you feel self-conscious about it?

How have you grown in your own walk of faith? Do you do things now (attend Bible study, pray with others, etc.) that you would not have when you first became a Christian?

How have your charted the milestones in your own journey of faith?

In what ways can you continue to grow in your faith?

Why is religion considered a taboo subject with the general public? How does this affect our attitude about sharing our faith with others?

How can we as Christians share about our faith without being offensive or condescending?

Reading Between the Lines

Keep.

Toss.

Donate.

I've seen enough home organization shows on HGTV to know this is my rule of thumb. Yet still, as my eyes take in my surroundings, I feel the weight of this job. I'm not just cleaning out a house; I am dismantling lives, the lives of my parents.

Mom passed away earlier this year, and Dad has moved into assisted living. We have chosen to rent the house, and cleaning it out is a final step in what has been a very taxing year. I should be happy for the closure, ready to move on. But surprisingly, as my work sets in, I discover emptying this house is like emptying my heart.

I look around the room with a new set of eyes. The furniture, the paintings on the wall, the antique table in the corner that displays a silver tea set. Almost everything in the house was my mother's. Dad's few collections and favorite things were relegated to the back porch.

As I walk through the house, I take it all in as if for the first time. The antique settee and lowboy we've had since I was a child, the marble coffee tables, the paintings lining the walls. Scenes of Venice, Indiana farmland, Vermont in the winter: each painting tells a bit about the places my mother loved. Most everything from my childhood remains in this room, though some of the furnishings marking my journey in faith—the black, white and green plaid couch from our old basement, the white couch and loveseat from my teen years—these were long gone.

Keep.

Toss.

Donate.

It is not as easy as the TV shows portray. I wander into the den and find my mother's bookshelves. For as much as she complained about Dad having too much stuff, she may have had more. The shelves are lined with books on art and literature and multiple biographies.

I walk over to them, run my fingers along the edges. My mother was an English teacher and an avid reader. These books are an extension of her. My oldest daughter shares her love for literature, so I decide to start here. I will save a few books for Sarah and some for me, and the rest can be donated to the local library. I begin to shuffle through the books, my keep, toss and donate piles set out before me. Then I see it. Wedged between Chaucer's *Canterbury Tales* and Flannery O'Connor's *The Habit of Being* is a small red record book. I know immediately it is one of my mother's journals.

A chill runs through me. Should I open it? Read it? To do so is not just an invasion of privacy, but also a risk. My mother could be critical; there's a chance I'll find words that sting. But instantly I envision her. It was just last spring when she and I were standing right here in this room. She'd been looking for a book she wanted to give me and came across a journal. "Oh, these journals. They are all over the house," she chuckled. "Someone is going to have a heyday reading about me when I'm gone."

My mother kept journals her entire adult life. Like me, she must have found solace in pouring her thoughts out onto the open page. But unlike me, she appeared not to be too concerned about anyone reading her most intimate thoughts. If I were she, a woman with a terminal illness and an unsure future, I'd have gathered up my journals and thrown them out. The thought of anyone reading my journals brings with it a sense of panic. I already have a pact with my best friend: the day I die she is to come to my house and burn them.

Should I read it? I think she wouldn't mind. But what do I really know about my mother? We were close for sure, but like many mothers and daughters, our relationship could be complex. A feisty woman, my mother was quick to express her disapproval. My response as a child was to retreat when she did so. As I got older I simply didn't risk sharing my most intimate thoughts with her. Though in these last years we had opportunities to talk more intimately, I never allowed myself to get completely vulnerable with her.

I stare down at the book in my hand and wonder whether I can handle what lies in these pages. While the adult me knew my mother loved and was very proud of me, it took me a long time to believe it. Reading harsh words from the past could easily stir up a load of emotions. What did she really think of me? Was she really proud? Did she like me as a person? These pages could certainly reveal her truth. Was I mature enough emotionally to understand, to put myself in her shoes, now that I too was a mother?

I close my eyes and randomly flip to the middle page of her journal. August 24, 1991. It is the day I got engaged to my now-husband Steve. Was she happy about the engagement? Did she like Steve? All I have to do is read to find out. My eyes are faster than my conscious mind, and before I know it I am reading:

Tracy and Steve got engaged. He took her to dinner at Dalt's, then rented a limo and in the limo he proposed. She accepted and he gave her a beautiful diamond ring. They came by the house and asked our blessing! Steve did this with style. I am pleased and think they will be a good match.

Relief. A tug on my heart. The courage to continue reading. Maybe her words can help me in my quest to better understand my mother, or myself.

I give up on the keep, toss, donate and instead go on a journal hunt. I spend the remainder of the afternoon searching for and collecting my mother's journals. I place them together in a box, and that evening, after everyone is asleep, I open the box and pore over her words. There are journals from when I was tiny, journals from my teen years and many journals written after I'd left for college.

Despite my fears, there are only neutral or positive comments about me. Mostly she wrote about her life, feelings and hopes for the future. Surprisingly her words echo those I'd written in my own journal.

Like me, my mother had insecurities, challenges and trouble balancing home and work (whatever made me think she didn't?). Like me, she sometimes wanted more, but loved her family fiercely and knew she couldn't have it all. I discover her struggles with keeping her marriage in a happy place and her worries about raising strong, independent children. Her words echo my own:

How can I get organized? How can I get help from this family? I shouldn't have to bear the burden of this house alone. I want to work full time but how can I knowing the situation as it is?

Suddenly I wonder if I knew this woman at all. The mother I grew up with was always so confident, so happy in her career. I never knew her to worry about housekeeping or getting it all done. Is it possible we have more in common than I thought? If I'd known her as a woman, instead of as my mother, would we have been friends?

Most surprising for me is learning the depths of my mother's faith:

Have been reading the Bible—Romans—Paul's letters and relearning, remembering in God's eyes it is believing, not achieving that counts. We are saved by our faith, through the grace of God, manifested in the act of Christ's sacrifice for us. I have trouble remembering that.

*I keep thinking that I must do something—be worth-
while. But in spiritual growth outward acts do not save
us. "First, seek ye the kingdom of God" say the scriptures.
All that we are to do will be revealed if we pay attention.
Being prayerful and reading the scriptures sincerely and
privately. It should not be a display. I guess I prefer that
it be private.*

My mother, who never bothered with church for
the majority of her life, who never spoke of God or
religion unless she was criticizing "the evangelicals,"
the woman who had daggers in her eyes when I told
her I was born again at age fifteen, carried within her
a deep, strong faith in God. I have mined what feels
like an extraordinary family secret.

I continue to read and find more:

*I have put in my application to become an oblate with
the Anglican monastery in Lexington, KY. The program
sounds very interesting. I'm waiting to hear from Brother Donald. I'm supposed to pray twice daily and read and
study. I look forward to the program and to the required
spiritual retreat (annual). I think it will be helpful in my
spiritual growth. I have read the Cloud of Unknowing
and loved it. It's about Christian contemplation. I want
to learn more about the development of these powers.*

My mother was an oblate. I did not know what it
was; I had to research it. An oblate is a layperson who
has specifically affiliated with a monastic community, someone who has dedicated himself to serving
God. I am stunned. Why didn't she ever talk about

this? Why did she keep her faith so private? Was she afraid, and if so, of what? What would my faith journey have looked like had we talked about our shared faith in God?

As I look back on my faith journey, I see imprints of my mother all over it. My desire to lean in to God and discover his love for me, my misunderstandings about my relationship with my mother, my confusion over what faith should look and feel like: all of this comes in some form from my mother.

So much I didn't understand. As a child, I longed to be in a family that went to church. I wanted to talk about my faith, to know what my parents' beliefs were, to understand more about God. But it was not a subject we ever discussed.

There was a period in my mother's life when she attended church; it was after I was in college. Is this when she became more serious with her faith? Is this when she became an oblate? Did she ever attend a spiritual retreat? I will never have the answers to these questions.

I want to be mad at my mother for not sharing her faith. I want to know why she felt the need to keep it private. I want to know what my journey would have been like had she shared her faith with me.

But while I want to, I can't be angry or blame my mother or even question why things are they way they are. I know God accomplishes his will in whatever way he wants to. It is not for me to understand or question. It's only up to me to trust.

Perhaps my mother had her own reasons for keeping her faith private. Perhaps her faith has been revealed to me at just the right time. Perhaps I should be grateful to now understand just how much her faith meant to her.

DISCUSSION QUESTIONS
Reading Between the Lines

In cleaning out her parents' home, the author finds and reads her mother's journal. In doing so, she discovers the depth of her mother's faith.

Was it right or wrong for the author to read her mother's journals?

Are Christians called to be public with their faith? Is there a right or wrong way to express one's faith?

What makes us vary in how we express our faith?

Has another person's expression of faith inspired you in your faith walk?

How much is hidden, secreted away, in our knowledge of those closest to us? Is there a way to break down the barriers, or should we even try to do this? Would pressing for inner thoughts be an invasion of privacy? Is the distancing in some ways a buffer?

Paul's letters and the understanding that faith is given, not earned, is discussed in this essay. If acts of goodness do not earn us a spot in heaven, why are Christian values and ideals important to uphold?

How do the impressions we receive as a child affect our adult thoughts and decisions? How can we accept our parents' views on faith if they are very different from our own?

What outside influences, cultural or otherwise, contribute to the ways in which we reveal our faith?

Acknowledgments

In 1975, sitting on a mat in the corner of Mrs. Jones's fourth grade classroom, I read Judy Blume's *Are You There God, It's Me Margaret?*, and thought to myself, I want to write books. My next thought was this: You could never do that. It took nearly 40 years to prove myself wrong. I could not have done it without the help of God and my very patient, very encouraging family and friends. I would like to thank the following people for contributing to both my walk in faith and my walk in writing:

My family: Steve, Sarah, Megan and Abby; Mom, Dad, Kent and Grandma 'Cille.

My friends: Susie, Rene, Marcia, Shelley, the GNO girls and all my friends of faith who have mentored me in so many ways.

My writing mentors: Lyn Jones, Nancy Baxter and those of you who've read and critiqued various parts of this book. Thank you.

And of course, God Himself.